D1558002

Paths of the Ancients...

APPALACHIA

Myths, Legends, and Landscapes of the Southern Highlands

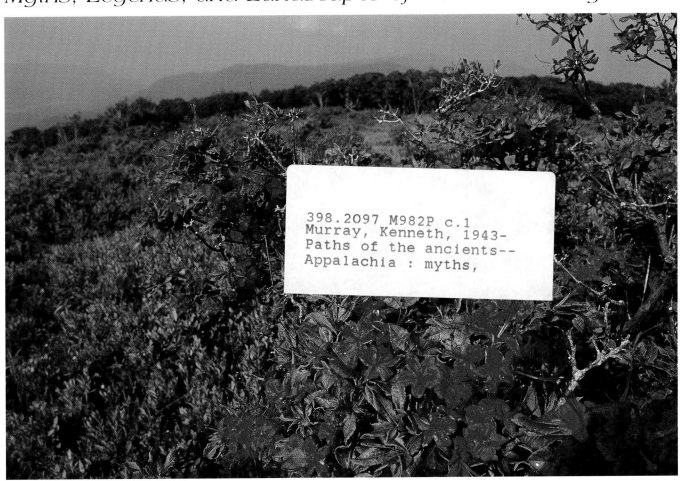

Kenneth Murray

Wild flame azaleas bloom on Gregory Bald.

The Overmountain Press
JOHNSON CITY, TENNESSEE

—OTHER BOOKS BY KENNETH MURRAY—

DOWN TO EARTH—PEOPLE OF APPALACHIA
A PORTRAIT OF APPALACHIA
HIGHLAND TRAILS—A Guide to Scenic Walking and Riding Trails (Revised 1992)**
Footsteps of the Mountain Spirits—APPALACHIA **

** Also available from The Overmountain Press

A nationally-acclaimed photographer, Kenneth Murray's work has been widely exhibited and published. His photographs have appeared in *Time, New York Times, People, Wilderness* and publications of the Appalachian Trail Conference, as well as other magazines and newspapers. A native of the Appalachian region, Murray's love of the highlands led to his quest to find and photograph the essence of the region's natural beauty. The above listed **Highland Trails** grew from a desire to share not only those photographs but the joy of that experience. This collection of stories and landscape photographs joins his photographic essays of the region's people and is a sequel to **Footsteps of the Mountain Spirits...APPALACHIA,** also published by The Overmountain Press. The myths, legends and regional lore found within this volume will be a treasured keepsake for those who love the Southern Highlands and a spiritual link between our diminishing natural world and those who passed this way before.

The Overmountain Press offers a variety of publications that preserve the heritage of the mountain region. A catalogue of current books is available from The Overmountain Press at P.O. Box 1261, Johnson City, TN 37605.

Late summer wildflowers blow in a light breeze on Little Hump Mountain in Tennessee, with Grassy Ridge and the Highlands of Roan in the background.

It was pleasant enough to lie here alone in the forest and be free! Aye, it was good to be alive, and to be far, far away from the broken bottles and old tin cans of civilization.

—Horace Kephart,
Our Southern Highlanders, 1913.

Story of The First Woman
A Catawba Genesis Myth

There was a time when the world was an unbroken waste of rocks, hills, and mountains, save only one small valley, which was distinguished for its luxuriance, and where reigned a perpetual summer. At that time, too, the only human being who inhabited the earth was a woman, whose knowledge was confined to this valley, and who is remembered among the Catawbas as the mother of mankind. She lived in a cavern, and her food consisted of the honey of flowers, and the sweet berries and other fruits of the wilderness. Birds without number, and the wild streams which found a resting-place in the valley, made the only music which she ever heard. Among the wild animals, which were very numerous about her home, she wandered without any danger; but the beaver and the doe were her favorite companions. In personal appearance she was eminently beautiful, and the lapse of years only had a tendency to increase the brightness of her eyes and the grace of her movements. The dress she wore was made of those bright green leaves which enfold the water lilies, and her hair was as long as the grass which fringed the waters of her native vale. She was the ruling spirit of a perennial world, for even the very flowers which bloomed about her sylvan home were never known to wither or die. In spite of her lonely condition, she knew not what it was to be lonely; but ever and anon a strange desire found its way to her heart, which impelled her to explore the wild country which surrounded her home. For many days had she resisted the temptation to become a wanderer from her charming valley, until it so happened, on a certain morning, that a scarlet butterfly made its appearance before the door of her cave, and by the hum of its wings invited her away. She obeyed the summons, and followed the butterfly far up a rocky ravine, until she came to the foot of a huge waterfall, when she was deserted by her mysterious pilot, and first became acquainted with the emotion of fear. Her passage of the ravine had been comparatively smooth; but when she endeavored, in her consternation, to retrace her steps, she found her efforts unavailing, and fell to the ground in despair. A deep sleep then overcame her senses, from which she was not awakened until the night was far spent; and then the dampness of the dew had fallen upon her soft limbs, and for the first time in her life did she feel the pang of a bodily pain. Forlorn and desolate indeed was her condition, and she felt that some great event was about to happen, when, as she uncovered her face and turned it to the sky, she beheld, bending over her prostrate form, and clothed in a cloud-like robe, the image of a being somewhat resembling herself, only that he was more stoutly made, and of a much fiercer aspect. Her first emotion at this strange discovery was that of terror; but as the mysterious being looked upon her in kindness, and raised her lovingly from the ground, she confided in his protection, and listened to his words until the break of day.

He told her that he was a native of the far off sky, and that he had discovered her in her forlorn condition while travelling from the evening to the morning star. He told her also that he had never before seen a being so soft and beautifully formed as she. In coming to her rescue he had broken a command of the Great Spirit, or the Master of Life, and, as he was afraid to return to the sky, he desired to spend his days in her society upon earth. With joy did she accept his proposal; and, as the sun rose above the distant mountains, the twain returned in safety to the luxuriant vale, where, as man and woman, for many moons, they lived and loved in perfect tranquillity and joy.

In process of time the woman became a mother; from which time the happiness of the twain became more intense, but they at the same time endured more troubles than they had ever known before. The man was unhappy because he had offended the Master of Life, and the mother was anxious about the comfort and happiness of her newly-born child. Many and devout were the prayers they offered the Great Spirit for his guidance and protection, for they felt that from them were to be descended a race of beings more numerous than the stars of heaven. The Great Spirit had compassion on these lone inhabitants of the earth; and, in answer to their prayers, he caused a mighty wind to pass over the world, making the mountains crowd closely together, and rendering the world more useful and beautiful by the prairies and valleys and rivers which now cover it, from the rising to the setting sun. The Master of Life also told his children that he would give them the earth and all that it contained as their inheritance; but that they should never enjoy their food without labor, should be annually exposed to a season of bitter cold, and that their existence should be limited by that period of time when their heads should become as white as the plumage of the sway....

—*Charles Lanman,*
Adventures in the Wilds of the United States and British American Provinces*, 1856.*

Whitewater Falls, one of the highest in the eastern United States, on the North Carolina/South Carolina border.

The preceding portrait of Eden was drawn from the origin myths of the Catawba Indians. It is set against the background of fertile valleys and rolling foothills overlooked by the eastern slopes of the Blue Ridge Mountains, in today's North and South Carolina. In that pristine world the features of the land and the forces of

Nature were intimately woven into the traditions of the Catawba, Cherokee, Creek, Tuscarora, and numerous other groups that roamed the Southern Highlands. Explorers and pioneers then added their heroic passages to the landscape. Through this lore the mountains speak across the centuries of ancient times and people gone before. They tell of events, both real and imagined, of heroes and fools and of a spiritual bond with the earth that seems like a dream when compared with today's frenzied rush for instant gratification and conspicuous consumption.

When the human tribe began its wanderings through the highlands of Southern Appalachia is not known. It may have been 12,000 years ago, or more. Who those first explorers were is equally obscure. Archaic relics such as arrow and spear points and other evidence of their long occupation is still turned up by plows, erosion, and archaeologists throughout the valleys and plains, millennia after their passing.

The world they inhabited, or even the one described in native American traditions and by early European wayfarers, defies imagination. There are few remaining places on Earth for comparison. Daniel Boone called the untouched wilderness beyond the Blue Ridge a "Second Paradise." John James Audubon described a single flock of American pigeons (now extinct) that contained more than one billion birds. This single flock required three hours to cross the Ohio River near Louisville, Kentucky, and blocked the sun as during an eclipse. The migration of one flock after another went on for several days. James Robertson, an early settler in the Watauga and Holston River valleys of Northeast Tennessee and Southwest Virginia, told of great herds of bison, deer, and elk (the southeastern elk, now extinct) that appeared from a distance to be one great pulsating beast. The numberless herds flowed over the plains and valleys like wide rivers. There were vast grassy plains and cane-brakes throughout the valleys. Many of the mountain crests, as along the Bald and Iron Mountains, were expanses of native grasses, blueberry bushes, and flowering rhododendron and azalea gardens, spanning much of the highland region from Virginia to northern Georgia.

The forests were equally inspiring. Dominated by the American chestnut, second only to the redwood in stature among American trees, the high vaulted canopy blocked the sun from the forest floor to create a park-like appearance. With the climax growth of Appalachian hardwoods on the slopes, gigantic pines on the lower plains, and spruce, fir, and northern adapted trees on the high crest, passing through the forest was compared to walking in God's greatest cathedral. An imported blight attacked the chestnut early this century and wiped out all but a few of the species. This loss, essentially of the entire species, ranks as one of the great botanical disasters of history. Other varieties are currently threatened by other man-made or man-intensified calamities, such as the Fraser fir, attacked by the imported balsam wooly aphid; the oaks, by the imported gypsy moth; the white pine by the southern pine bark beetle; and numerous others by acid rain deposition and other air- and water-borne pollutants.

It is difficult to imagine the lives of the forest nations residing within this primeval world. A persistent romantic view of this vanquished past is that of the noble prince of the forest living in complete harmony with the bountiful mother earth, reverent and respectful of the ancient spirits and unseen forces of the environment, living in tolerance with all fellow creatures. But it must also have been a harsh and unmerciful place, filled with hardship, uncertainty, danger, and cruel and constant warfare. There was chronic fighting among neighboring groups.

Dozens of mutually unintelligible languages were spoken, but many traits and ideals were held in common. Property was not accumulated or passed from generation to generation in the forest cultures; therefore, an individual's standing in society was based on merit. Emphasis was on maintaining a personalized relationship with the intangible forces that gave structure and meaning to life. Living was a contemplative, religious experience, and much time was spent in establishing harmony with all existence.

James Adair (an early British trader among the Creek, Cherokee, Chickasaw, and others) advocated the idea that the woodland groups of the Southeast were descended from the Hebrews and offered a substantial body of evidence to support his viewpoint. This idea has been largely discounted in recent years, but the intricate value systems, where crime and selfishness were nearly nonexistent, were also suggested as model societies by several early wayfarers, including the Quaker botanist William Bartram. There were numerous instances of early explorers, traders, and adventurers forsaking the benefits of European privilege and civilization to join aboriginal groups.

One major flaw in native societies was the constant and brutal warring. Exploits in war were the primary ways for young men to attain status within their tribes. In most groups they were treated as children, or with contempt and forced servitude, until they had some form of the title "Man Killer" added to their names. Other disadvantages became apparent when facing the challenge from white invaders, such as their inability to present a united front. Intertribal rivalries and imported diseases, for which they had no resistance, hastened their dispossession.

Most encounters between native American tribes and Europeans were marked by mutual contempt and inhumanity. Indians regarded the white men as godless barbarians, with an unexplainable hunger for gold and silver, who even thought they could own the earth from which man had come and all must return. Many native American tribes encountered by colonial land

A bed of yellow Toadshade Trillium carpets the forest floor near Whitewater Falls, along the North Carolina/South Carolina border.

speculators and explorers, such as William Byrd, had intricate and sophisticated religious systems, rivaling the mystic tenets of the Far East disciplines, with intricate ideas of reincarnation and the existence of parallel worlds in time and space. Many believed that those who had lived virtuous lives passed quickly to a bright and happy world of plenty after death. But those who had not, or whose wrongful death had not been avenged, might remain in limbo or be returned to Earth to try it again. Another belief held that the present Earth had been preceded by several others that have existed in the dreams of the Great Spirit. He Who Lives Above became tired of His earlier creations and forgot them when their people became corrupt, or had not cared for the world He had given them.

The Indian was generally referred to by the Whites as heathen savages with only superstitious beliefs—therefore, fodder for conversion to Christian enlightenment, enslavement, or commitment to eternity. The barbarity of absolutist religious dogma to justify unconscionable conquest is a dominant theme of human history.

The expedition of Hernando de Soto was probably the first to bring European ideals to the Appalachian highlands. De Soto had become a wealthy man through the defeat and armed robbery of the Inca of Peru. When this army of around 1,000 men and one woman (the woman had disguised herself as a man until the expedition was underway) marched through the Southeast, de Soto was the appointed Governor of all the unknown territories he explored. His mission was to reconnoiter for new lands to colonize and natives to convert, as well as to perform immediate exploitation. Although he was experienced in the lofty Andes of South America, by the time the foothills of the Southern Appalachians were reached, the expedition was experiencing great difficulties. They had discovered little booty and had considerable dissent within the troop. Their trip through the highlands was mostly uneventful, and landmarks given by chroniclers of the journey are vague. But by the time the army reached the Tennessee Valley, the common soldiers had learned to use their chain mail to sift corn flour to cook Indian fry bread and tortillas and to live off the land. There had probably been several desertions from indentured soldiers.

The exact route this expedition took through the mountains in the summer of 1540 is still debated by students of the subject. After advancing up the Georgia coastal plain and piedmont, perhaps as far as Augusta, Georgia, or Columbia, South Carolina, the procession turned toward the inland passes. Two of the more likely routes were along aboriginal trading/war paths through the Hiwassee or Little Tennessee River valleys. If either of these was the actual route, the army then took a meandering course down the Tennessee Valley, through northern Georgia, Alabama, and Mississippi, then on to explore parts of Arkansas, Texas, and Louisiana. En route the conquistadors were essentially defeated by the Alabamu and the Chickasaw tribes. At least one soldier threw away several pounds of pearls to lighten his load. Eventually they ran out of powder for their guns and melted them down to make nails for building rafts to continue their journey. The expedition was finally reduced to starvation and malaria.

From this time it is probable that the mountain region was under Spanish influence for around 150 years. Most of their activities were closely guarded secrets, although remnants of their mining works have been found in the Carolinas and Georgia.

Another Spanish expedition that was partially recorded was that of Juan Pardo. He marched his force up the watershed of either the Santee or Peedee River in South Carolina to about the present site of Columbia. From here he established manned inland outposts, probably across the foothills of Georgia and Alabama. He had been instructed to develop good relations with the indigenous peoples and develop a land link to New Spain (Mexico). But shifting priorities forced abandonment of the forts he had established, and the fates of the

A butterfly feeds on wild flame azalea blooms on Gregory Bald along the crest of the Great Smoky Mountains in Tennessee.

men who manned them is uncertain. It is probable that many retraced their routes back to the coast and that others joined the natives. Popular speculation attributes the origin of the mountain people known as "Melungeons" to these abandoned Spanish soldiers, or to deserters from the de Soto expedition. A few desertions from de Soto, and those left behind due to illness, were recorded, such as two soldiers who left the mission somewhere in the mountain region.

De Soto had forced an Indian queen or princess, who apparently had influence from the Georgia coastal plains to the head waters of the Savannah River, to accompany his troop inland. Things went well for a few days, but then the queen escaped and two of the soldiers went with her to become her husbands.

By the middle of the 1600s there was great rivalry between the European powers to establish their influence and trade in North America. Most of the current perspective comes from the English since they emerged as winners of the competition. But for more than one hundred years the French were the dominant force west of the Blue Ridge. They established a trading network along most of the inland rivers and had the loyalty of many of the woodland tribes. But loyalties were frequently awarded to the French, Spanish, or the English along the lines of long-time Indian rivalries. A tribe would join the side that would aid them against their traditional enemies. The French established several forts and outposts along the river valleys to support their trade and to instigate disfavor against the British. This agitation culminated in the conflict known as the French and Indian War. Generally, the French had better relations with the Indians than did the British, since the English were perceived as more likely to intrude on Indian lands. But this was not always the case. In trying to establish themselves in the Chickasaw country, the French ran into stiff resistance and were forced to withdraw. In one encounter recorded by Adair, the Chickasaw defeated a French army of 1,500.

The relentless push of farmers inland from the Atlantic coastal plain had begun, along with the pattern of wars and treaties that eventually reached the Pacific coast. In these conflicts tribes such as the Cherokee joined in the decimation of their traditional enemies such as the Catawba, Tuscarora, Creek, Shawnee, and others. From that time a new era began in the mountains with the intrepid pioneer partly absorbing and displacing those earlier on the land, just as tribe had displaced tribe in the past.

There was a conflicting ethic between the Indian tribes and European immigrants who poured across the mountains following the American Revolution. Supported by their religion, the pioneer considered any piece of land not under plow to be a wasteland or desert. It was believed to be their God-given mandate to conquer the Earth and bring it into cultivation. The great forest was cut and hauled away where convenient, or, more frequently, burned to get it out of the way. It was believed, as late as the early part of this century, that the great forest was so vast that it would be impossible to ever cut it all. John James Audubon and other early conservationists expressed the belief that hunting of the innumerable flocks of American pigeons or herds of buffalo would have little or no effect on their survival. This attitude was taken with other resources of the region as well, to the point that actual wastelands of abandoned strip mines and clear-cut forests are now common.

The exploitation and decline of the dream-like perfection that was Appalachia were the results of inevitable and irresistible forces brought by the exploding population of the human species. Pressures to overwhelm the last of the natural environment will most likely increase.

Ironically, the mountaineer whose family immigrated to the highlands generations ago—drawn by the independence and solitude the region offered, and their own lands to supply their needs—may find the beauty and productivity of the mountains, its streams and air, destroyed by the new land rush.

Again, the few will make great profits selling the heritage of the many who love the mountains but would not join a united front to protect them.

It is a perception of beauty. For some, the sight of neat rows of second-home chalets, all with 50-foot motor homes and Lincolns tethered to the back, parked behind security gates, with "No trespassing" notices, embellishing every ridge line is beauty. Others take pride in the efficient removal of every tree from the forest, although the practice has been proven unsustainable,

The Dark Hollow area of the Shenandoah National Park in Virginia.

or the removal of every lump of coal, whatever the environmental or human cost.

What value and what priority is merited by the shrinking natural Appalachia? Where is the next frontier? Where will your children go for a pure mountain vista? It is a matter of values.

Explanations of the forces of the natural world and passing events were presented in poetic and fanciful dress by Indian orators and by the unlettered mountaineers who followed them into the Southern Appalachian region. The rich tapestry of myths, legends, and folklore continues as a strong influence in the mountains, although the stories are now tempered by print and immediacy of the electronic media.

This book presents a selection of this lore, observations of early travelers, related historical settings, events, and characters. Sometimes the factual accounts are as entertaining and implausible as the fiction. Many of the stories have been retold from older sources.

In times past, the telling of one of the myths might have required great ritual and an entire evening, or even days, to relate. The hearing of myths and legends, interpreting of dreams, fasting, and prayers to the Ones Above for guidance were once the beginnings of individual vision quests, or initiation into the realm of the spiritual. The stories served as examples and guides for the inner quest through an intricate web of stories within stories that take seemingly divergent paths through the imagination. The world of delight that still exists in the small percentage of unspoiled Appalachia can still be a bridge for the journey between the inner spiritual world and the outer journey along landscapes that inspire and evoke new tales of wonder.

There is still a great hunger for initiation into the mysteries and meaning of one's own life and one person's obligations to all life. Expression of this hunger may be seen by one person walking the 2,100 miles of the Appalachian Trail in a season, or the travel of another to exotic lands and cultures. The hunger for the vision quest remains, but there are few guides for the journey. For many, the relics to inspire the spiritual journey are held in man-made temples or museums. But for others, the places where the inner and outer journeys join is in the world as it was created.

It seems unlikely that any of the Creators, however individually named or perceived, would condone the destruction of the last of their invention.

Whatever the nature of the Gods, they seem nearer along the exalted ridges of the highlands. The magic of a timeless Appalachia may be found along emerald hollows, or while listening to the music of a waterfall. The pulse of the Earth may be felt along throbbing, rocky streams. Even for the cynic there is an unexplainable presence, an elation and exhilaration to be felt while walking along the summits of this vibrant natural world. A soul touching, spiritual sensation may be felt along the open balds and crests of places like the Shining Rock Wilderness, Grayson Highlands, the crest of the Smokies, or summits of the Roan Highlands. A few unspoiled power points remain: places where clouds sweep across boundless horizons, like fragments of a time lapse dream; places where a sunburst skips along the ridges, appearing like a great scrim on the vast stage of "He Who Gives Breath," to create highlights that shift the focus from foreground trees and coneflowers to blue/green vanishing points.

Later, after the Sun has completed Its day's march across the sky and the last of the afterglow passes from lonely hill crests, in the thin, clear air, the sea of stars begins a dance across the heavens to reveal the "Road of the Spirits," as the Milky Way was known to earlier wayfarers. It beckons as a well-traveled path for the journey that we all must make, with joy, in uncertainty, or in fear. Faded highlights of earthly paths, lacing across the summits and through the vaulted arches of spruce, fir, and mountain ash, evoke an illusion of convergence near the horizon with the celestial trail of countless points of light and star dust leading on to an unknowable time and place for those on this shore. Here there is little reference, or even relevance, to the passage of time. One person's passage would be as a blink in the limitless universe; a nomad of centuries past would have watched with the same awe as today's wayfarer. Here the land of the sky is closer than anywhere in the man-made world. Here are the coastlines of the heavens.

Whatever there is that is sacred resides here. Here—with time briefly suspended, atop rocky knolls in the tentative flickers of morning light, heralded by the murmur of a rising breeze, the drone of the world spinning, the purl of our mother and father Earth hurtling through an infinite universe—a part of our incredible odyssey into the unknowable void begins. And perhaps here, in

Catawba Rhododendron bloom on the Highlands of Roan route of the Appalachian Trail near its junction with the Grassy Ridge Trail along the Tennessee/North Carolina border.

the same breeze that brings the floating incense from surrounding balsam woods, in the shimmering dew that refreshes the grasses, or in the mica-flecked dust of the rocky path, there will be a whispered remembrance of the ephemeral passage of you and of me along the aisles of this alpine cathedral, where the sharp tops reach for the heavens like rock-clad steeples. And may we be weighed worthy on these paths to join the aura of gentle spirits, yearning and hopeful, to keep a mystic watch with those who passed, with reverence and in awe, along this hallowed dreamscape of the ancients.

Autumn foliage along the slopes of Mount Mitchell, North Carolina.

The Catawba tribe occupied the foothills and piedmont areas northeast of the Cherokee in North and South Carolina. They were fierce fighters. The tribe had a custom of flattening a male infant's head by placing a sandbag on his forehead while on a cradle board, giving their warriors a particularly menacing appearance. This also forced the eyes farther apart, which they believed improved their marksmanship. The practice may actually have improved their depth perception slightly, an advantage when using a bow and arrow or hand-thrown spear. The tribe was nearly wiped out by wars and disease during the colonial era, and most of the survivors joined the removal west before and during the "Trail of Tears," although a small group remained in the East. They are remembered in the names of several regional landmarks, and the most brightly colored variety of rhododendron, the Catawba Rhododendron, bears their name.

How the Earth Came to Be
An Iroquois Genesis Myth

Long ago and far away, a race of gigantic anthropic beings dwelt in the skyland.

Here dwelt these first beings in peace and contentment for a very long period of time; no one knows or ever knew the length of this first cosmic period of tranquil existence. But the time came when an event occurred which resulted in a metamorphosis in the state and aspect of celestial and earthly things....

Into the sunless and moonless skyland, lighted only by the snowy white flowers of the great tree of light, standing high near the lodge of Dehaohwendji-awakho ("He the Earth Holder"), the presiding chief of that realm, jealousy crept. This chief, reputed to be invincible to sorcery, took a young wife by betrothal in fulfillment of a vision of his soul. The name of the young woman was Awehai, "Mature Flowers," or "Fertile Earth." Through the crafty machinations of the Fire Dragon of the White Body, the consuming jealousy of the aged presiding chief was kindled against his young spouse.

The bride became pregnant simply by inhaling the breath of her mate. The betrothed husband, not knowing the cause or source of her condition, questioned her chastity and with reluctance resolved within himself to expel from his lodge and land his suspected but innocent spouse.... The disturbed state of his mind caused him to have another vision of his soul. In fulfillment of the requirements of this vision he caused the tree of light, then standing over the supposed aperture through which the sun now shines, to be uprooted, whereby there was formed an abyss into the empyrean of this world. By craft he succeeded in thrusting his unsuspecting young spouse into this abyss....

The expelled bride, Awehai, while floating through cosmic space of the upper sky, was seen in her descent by the waterfowl and water animals of the primal sea...[and they] at once set themselves the task of providing a habitation for her.... The waterfowl of the larger kinds flew up to meet her and to bring her slowly down as she rested on their united backs. While this was being done the best divers among the water animals brought up from the depths of the sea some wet earth, which was carefully placed on the carapace of the Great Turtle....

This wet earth at once began to expand in size in all directions, and on it Awehai was gently placed. At once she began to walk about the tiny earth, and by this action she caused it to continue to grow in size; she even took handfuls of the earth and scattered it in all directions, which likewise caused it to continue to expand until it had grown so large that she could no longer see its bounds. Then shrubs, red willow, grasses, and other vegetation began to appear.

In the fullness of time she gave birth to a daughter. After attaining womanhood this daughter was courted by various man-beings and other beings disguised in the assumed shape of fine-looking young men. But, by her mother's advice, she rejected the suit of all until a young man of the race of the Great Turtle sought her to wife....

In due time the young woman gave birth to twins, one of whom caused her death by violently bursting through her armpit. The name of the culprit twin was Ohaa, and that of his brother, the elder, was Dehaehiyawakho.

The grandmother was enraged by this and asked who had killed her daughter. Ohaa accused his innocent brother who the grandmother cast into the shrubbery and hated bitterly from that time.

man, the human being, whom later he was to create. For ease of transit for man Dehaehiyawakho had made the rivers and streams with double currents, the one current running upstream and the other running downstream; but his brother changed this well-intentioned device by putting falls and cascades in the rivers and streams. The grandmother, seeing that Dehaehiyawakho had produced great ears of perfect corn, immediately blighted them and said, "You desire the human beings you are about to make to be too happy and too well provided with necessities."

The elder twin continued to make all the good things of earth, while his grandmother and younger brother continued to spoil them in some degree, so that the people would have to struggle for a living. Seeing the futility of continuing this way they finally decided to determine who would control the nature of things by a dice game, and when the elder won, Dehaehiyawahko became the Master of Life.

Dehaehiyawakho was an imaginary man-being of the cosmogonic philosophy of the Iroquoian and other American mythologies. He was, in brief, the symbolic embodiment or personification of all earthly life, floral and faunal. The wise men of the elder time attributed to him the formation or creation and conservation of life and the living things in normal and beneficent bodies and things in terrestrial nature.

The story of the Earth-Grasper, the Elder One, or the Master of Life, with numerous variations, was common to most of the Iroquoian language group, which included the Seneca, Cherokee, and Tuscarora. This version is from the ***Forty-third Annual Report of the Bureau of American Ethnology to the Secretary of the Smithsonian Institution***, 1928. Accompanying paper by J.B.N. Hewitt, *Iroquoian Cosmology*.

Dark Hollow Falls in the Big Meadows area of the Shenandoah National Park in Virginia.

But he did not die, and as the twins grew they each began to create the things that would be placed into the world.

Dehaehiyawakho labored to prepare the earth for

A winter view west from the Appalachian Trail in the Peaks of Otter region of Virginia.

The Morning Star and the Cannibal Wife
A Seneca Legend

Once, far off in the woods, there lived by themselves a husband and wife. It was the custom of the husband to hunt, while the woman devoted her time to raising corn and beans.

One day, while the wife was baking a cake in the ashes, a large spark from the fire fell on her hand.

Late summer ferns and blackberry bushes line a path on Spruce Knob in West Virginia, in the southern range of the Seneca tribe.

The pain caused her to rub the spot with her finger, and putting it in her mouth, she tasted her own blood. Strange as it may seem, she took a liking to it and craved more. So with a knife she began to cut off parts of her flesh and ravenously ate it. Soon she had eaten all her arms and legs, but still could not stop.

Now the husband had a loyal dog and it was watching what the wife was doing, and when she was about halfway through eating the flesh off of her limbs, the unnatural wife turned to the dog and said, "You would better go and tell your friend and master to escape from this place at once, for if you do not hurry away, I shall eat you both." He ran as fast as he could into the forest and told the hunter what had happened, and that she would eat them both if they did not flee immediately. They started to run but after awhile the man, knowing that the dog's legs were short and not strong, suggested that he hide in a hollow tree. The dog consented but realized that he was sacrificing himself to save the man. He knew what was in store for them both and gave his life to delay the woman with her growing hunger. The man ran and ran until he came to a wide river which he could not cross without the help of the old man who lived there. He said, "Grandfather, I am in great trouble. Take me across the river to save me from peril of my life. My wife, who has become a cannibal, is pursuing me in order to devour me."

The old man replied: "Oh! I know what you are telling me, but she is still a long way behind you. She will not be here for some time to come. But you must bring me a basketful of fish from my fishpond." The hunter went to get the fish so the old man would help him.

The hunter caught the fish, and he and the old man cooked them up and ate them; then the old man helped him across the river and directed him where he might get further help on his journey.

Meanwhile back at their camp, the woman was finishing her meal, even to pushing the marrow out of her bones with a small stick to also eat that, so hungry was she. She then filled the hollows in her bones with small pebbles, which rattled as she moved around. From time to time she sang and danced, causing the pebbles in her bones to rattle, whereupon she would exclaim, "Oh, that sounds fine!"

Having become ravenous again she began to eat everything edible in sight, then set out following her husband's tracks. Once in a while she would stop in her fiendish pursuit to dance around a bit, listening with delight to the rattle of the small pebbles in her bones, then take up the trail again.

Coming to the bank of the river, she screamed, "Old man take me across this river. Come! Be Quick!" The old ferryman, not being accustomed to being talked to that way, delayed her as much as he could. He finally consented to let her cross, but he became so angry with her constant ranting that in midstream he caused her to fall into the river where she was quickly devoured by the monsters that dwelt there.

The man kept on running, fearing that he had not yet escaped, and indeed his troubles were not yet ended. Soon he came to a beautiful wood in which he saw a young woman gathering sticks for fuel. She asked, "Where are you going?"

He replied, "I am going on until I find pleasant people to live with."

The young woman answered, "You would better remain here with me as my husband. We can live very happily if you can manage my grandmother, who is a little old woman, but very troublesome." As the young woman was pleasant and good-looking, the hunter decided to remain with her. Arriving at the lodge of the two women, the grandmother, who was about half the height of a normal person but very stout, became very angry with the young woman and beat her unmercifully with a club, but finally relented. The old woman said that she would let the husband stay, but that the first night he would have to stay with her. During the night the old

The Judy Rocks formations in late summer rain in Monongahela National Forest in West Virginia. This was the southern range of the Seneca but also was claimed by the Mingo, Shawnee, Delaware, and others.

woman tried to smother and suffocate the hunter, but he was barely able to survive. For a time after that she left the young couple in peace to enjoy themselves.

Several days later the old woman brought out a canoe and said to the man, "We must go to an island today to hunt." On reaching the island she directed him to its far end where she would then drive the game toward him. He started for his position, but before he got very far he heard a sound behind him and turned to find the old woman gliding away rapidly in the canoe. He looked around the island and noticed dark rings on the tree trunks and realized he was in great trouble. Looking around, he chose the very tallest of the trees and began to climb. During the night the water in the river began to rise and soon covered all the island and continued to rise. The water kept rising and he continued to climb as it rose.

With the first streak of dawn in the east the hunter saw that all the shorter trees were covered with water, while around him on all sides were great numbers of monsters waiting to devour him. He sat at the top of the tree, looking for any avenue of escape. He saw the Morning Star shining brightly in the east and thought it might be time for him to sing his death song. But then he remembered that the Morning Star had promised him in a dream in the days of his youth to help him in the time of trouble or peril. He prayed that the Morning Star would hasten the coming of day, for he believed that with the advent of daylight the waters would subside and he would be saved. He cried in the anguish of his mind: "Oh, Morning Star! hasten the Orb of Day. Oh Morning Star! hurry on the daylight. You promised when I was young that you would help me if I ever should be in great peril."

Morning Star lived in a beautiful lodge and asked a servant, "Who is that shouting on the island?"

The boy replied, "Oh! that is the husband of the little old woman's granddaughter. He says you promised to help him in time of trouble."

Morning Star replied, "Oh, yes! I did promise him to do so. Let the Orb of Day come at once." And daylight came and the waters receded.

After the land dried, the hunter descended the tree and buried himself in the sand to hide. Soon the old woman returned In the canoe to see how he had fared during the night. Delighted to see that he seemed to not be on the island, she said to herself, "The flesh of my granddaughter's husband has been eaten up by this time, but I suppose his bones are left, and being very young, they must have good marrow in them, so I think I will have some of his marrow." So saying, she began to search the island. The man had been watching her, and as she crossed the island he jumped into the canoe and sped away. When she saw this she cried out in despair, "Oh, grandson, come back! I will never play another trick on you. I will love you." But the hunter replied, "You shall play no more tricks on me," and continued to paddle away.

When night came again the water began to rise and the old woman climbed a pine tree to escape. Between midnight and sunrise the water had nearly reached her, and she began to call to the Morning Star. "You promised you would help me when I should be in distress." Morning Star asked the boy, "Is the man down there on the island yet?" The lad replied, "Oh, no! He got off yesterday. This is the little old woman herself. She says you promised her in a dream to help her." But Morning Star replied, "Oh, no! I never made any promise to her." With these words the Morning Star fell asleep again and slept on, letting the Orb of Day come in its own time. The water on the island kept rising and rising until it reached the top of the pine and the little old lady disappeared.

The couple at home then lived in peace and happiness.

—*Retold from Jeremiah Curtin and J.N.B. Hewitt,* Seneca Fiction, Legends and Myths, *in the* **Thirty-Second Annual Report of the Bureau of American Ethnology to the Secretary of the Smithsonian Institution***, 1910-1911.*

The "Devil's Bathtub" on Devil's Fork of Stoney Creek in the Jefferson National Forest of Virginia. This is probably along the route followed by red-headed war chief Benge, and possibly by Mingo war chief Logan, when raiding settlements along the Clinch and North Holston valleys during the pioneer era.

Turtle and His Forces Go on the Warpath
A Seneca Legend

Turtle dwelt alone in his own lodge. He was a great warrior and had led many war parties successfully.

One day the thought again came to him that he should go on the warpath. So, following the lead of his desire, he made the necessary preparations, boarded his canoe, and paddled away along the river, singing as he went, "I am on the warpath. I am on the warpath."

When he had gone but a short distance he was hailed by someone who came running to the bank of the river calling out, "Hallo, friend! Stop a moment! I will go too. We will go on the warpath together." So Turtle stopped at the landing, and there on the bank stood an elk, which said, "I should like to go with you on the warpath."

Turtle replied: "Before giving my consent, I desire to see you run, for we might be defeated and then we shall have to run for our lives, and unless we can escape through our speed we shall be killed and scalped. Now, therefore, run to that mountain and return." Elk ran with great swiftness to the mountain and was back again in a very short time. But Turtle said, "You can not go, for you do not run fast enough. Only swift runners may go with me."

On he went singing, "I am on the warpath. I am on the warpath," and was soon hailed again. This time it was the skunk—again the test—but before he had gotten far Turtle called him back saying, "Come back; that is enough. You can go." So they got into the canoe and started off, Turtle singing, "I am on the warpath. I am on the warpath. But you, brother, smell quite strong."

Another hail, this time the porcupine—again the running test—but, in his attempt to dash, his feet got tangled and he fell, but Turtle stopped him and said, "You will do. Come to the canoe."

Turtle then continued his song, "We are on the warpath. You, brother, smell pretty strong. You, brother, have plenty of arrows."

Next the war party was hailed by the buffalo and then the rattlesnake. Buffalo went crashing through trees and brush, demolishing everything in his path, but on his return was told that he had failed the test. When Rattlesnake raised himself to run Turtle exclaimed, "Oh, you will do! You may come with me, too."

So the picked band of warriors set out singing "We

are on the warpath. You, brother, smell pretty strong. You, brother, have plenty arrows. And you, brother, have a black face."

It was near night and they were going to make war on the Seven Sisters, known for their evil witchcraft. Turtle told his warriors that each must position himself at the place best suited for his type of fighting. So Skunk declared that he would sit near the fireplace and that he would attack with his odors the first person who approached. Porcupine chose the woodpile and would attack anyone who came for fuel. Rattlesnake chose the bucket where the corn was kept. Turtle chose a place near the spring.

Next morning the mother of the Seven Sisters went to stir the fire and was attacked by foul odors; she fell back nearly stifled and unable to open her eyes. Her daughters, hearing the commotion, arose quickly to assist their mother. They killed Skunk with their war clubs and threw his body out of doors. Next, one went to the woodpile; and when she bent down, she felt a severe blow on her arm and found her arm full of hedgehog quills. She repelled the attack and her sisters came to her aid. They beat Porcupine to death with sticks of wood and threw his body away.

Then one of the sisters went to get some shelled corn for a meal and, putting her hand into the bucket, immediately felt a sharp blow and then saw the huge Rattlesnake. She called for help; and using clubs, they dispatched him and threw his body away, but by then the one bitten was dead.

The aged mother of the remaining sisters asked one of her daughters to go get some water from the spring; and when she bent down she was seized by Turtle. He grabbed her toe and held on persistently; she drug him back to the lodge to get help. Back at the lodge her mother became very angry and shouted, "Throw him into the fire and let him burn up."

Then Turtle laughed out loud and said, "You can not please me more than by casting me into the fire,

Patterns in an ancient sea or lake bed are revealed in the sandstone of the Natural Bridge area of Kentucky's Daniel Boone National Forest.

Winter along the Virginia Highlands Horse Trail, near Scales, in the Mount Rogers National Recreation Area, Virginia.

for I came from fire and I like to be in it rather than anything else."

So the old woman changed her mind and said, "I will take him to the creek and drown him."

Thereupon Turtle cried out in great agony, "Oh! do not do this. I shall die; I shall die if you do." He begged hard for his life, but it apparently availed him nothing. So the old woman and the six living sisters, seizing Turtle, ruthlessly dragged him to the creek and cast him into it, thinking that he would drown; he, of course, naturally sank to the bottom. But in a few moments he rose to the surface of the water in midstream; and holding out his claws as if exhibiting scalps, he exclaimed in derision, "I am a brave man, and here is where I live," and he at once sank out of sight.

—Retold from Jeremiah Curtin and J.N.B. Hewitt,
Seneca Fiction, Legends and Myths, *1910-1911.*

Settlement Era

The first European explorers crossing the high passes of the Allegheny Mountains discovered that the parallel valleys between the Blue Ridge crests and the Cumberland range were a vast no-man's-land. Used as a communal hunting ground by all the tribes brave enough to venture into the area, it was also a favorite place of ambush by the constantly warring bands. One tradition, possibly from Cherokee and Shawnee lore, explains the absence of permanent settlements in the rich valleys.

...In so favored a land, where man's natural wants are so fully satisfied, there could be no community of peace and happiness, that with such ease to the body and disquiet to the soul the councils of man must always overflow with the vanities of argument and the pride of innate egotism; so the tradition was, that once of old there was a delegated assemblage of the chiefs of the Indian tribes for a conference with the Great Spirit, at which conference the Great Spirit detailed certain great calamities that had befallen them in the paradise of Hogoheegee, which were traceable to the causes named above, and thereupon the Great Spirit ordered all their nations to remove beyond certain boundaries, out of this Eden, which the Great Spirit informed them was too easy of life for their content and happiness and their future security.

Thereupon this vast empire was consigned to the peaceful dominion of nature, and all the lands upon the waters from the Holston to the headwaters of the Kentucky and Cumberland rivers were without permanent inhabitants.

—Cited by Lewis Preston Summers
The History of Southwest Virginia, 1746-1786,
Washington County, 1777-1870*, 1903.*

Knowledge of the rich valleys between the Blue Ridge and Cumberland Mountains was common to traders, hunters, explorers, and land speculators by the middle of the 1700s. Urged on by men like Thomas Walker and William Byrd, outposts and settlers advanced down the Virginia valleys with little initial opposition from the surrounding tribes. Recorded journeys include a surveying expedition by Walker in 1749 that traveled beyond the Cumberland Gap and into the Kentucky region.

Around 1756 Daniel Boone led a hunting party over the mountains from North Carolina to Kentucky. Starting in the Yadkin Valley, the party followed aboriginal and game paths through today's Boone to Trade, on the Tennessee border, then down Taylor's Valley, where they spent the first night. The next day they hunted down the South Holston River to Wolf Hills (today's Abingdon, Virginia) where...**Daniel Boone and his companions, immediately after nightfall, were troubled by the appearance of great numbers of wolves, which assailed their dogs with such fury that it was with great difficulty**

Trillium and Fringed Phacelia carpet the forest floor in the Mount Rogers National Recreation Area, Virginia.

Spring wildflowers bloom (star chickweed and common blue violet) on the slopes of Whitetop Mountain, overlooking Taylor's Valley and the Laurel/Whitetop Gorge, Virginia.

that the hunters succeeded in repelling their attacks and saving the lives of their dogs, a number of which were killed or badly crippled by the wolves.

—*Cited by Lewis Preston Summers*
The History of Southwest Virginia, 1746-1786,
Washington County, 1777-1870*, 1903.*

During this and subsequent journeys across the mountains, Boone and other long hunters killed incredible numbers of deer and bear for trade skins. Boone alone recorded killing more than 2,500 deer and 100 bear in a season. The romantic, skirling "horn in the west" he was supposed to have heard, beckoning to rich lands beyond the Blue Ridge, might easily have been the haunting cry of the withering herds. Valleys were blanketed with bleaching bones and rotting carcasses stripped of their skins for trade. A trade rifle might cost 35 pelts, a blanket 15, or one skin might purchase a single mouthful of whiskey.

Regal forest and the wealth of millennia were swept before a tide of rifles, axes, and plows. But the mountain heartland must have seemed an inexhaustible larder of plenty, the promised land, a new kingdom of paradise, pristine Canaan, Bethel, or Eden, just waiting to be taken by eager settlers. Even conflicts with the natives were minor at first, since there seemed to be plenty for all.

But this would change.

On one of his journeys, in the summer of 1773, Boone met Captain William Russell, who had recently established a large plantation near Castlewood, Virginia, and agreed on a plan to lead a group of settlers into Kentucky.

The "White Rocks" overlook with the Cumberland Gap area in the background. White cliffs along this mountain, on the Kentucky/Virginia border, served as landmarks for pioneers traveling along the valley and the Wilderness Road.

The Deaths of James Boone and Henry Russell

In September of 1773 Boone started from the Yadkin Valley of North Carolina to a rendezvous point in Southwest Virginia. At Abingdon, Boone sent his son James, 16, along with Richard Mendenhall and his brother John of Gilford County, North Carolina, to Castlewood to inform Captain Russell that the settlers were on their way and to obtain a supply of flour and farming tools. At Castlewood they were joined by Russell's son Henry, 17, Isaac Crabtree, and two of Russell's slaves, Charles and Adam. Heavily loaded with supplies, they headed down the Clinch River, via Hunters Ford and Rye Cove, to rejoin the main party.

But they were overtaken by darkness before they reached the main party, waiting near present-day Stickleyville, Virginia, and camped about three miles in their rear. During the night wolves surrounded the camp and howled dismally, on which the Mendenhall brothers expressed fear and were twitted with cowardice by Isaac Crabtree, who jocularly told them that in Kentucky, the place to which they were going, they would hear wolves and buffaloes howling in the tree tops.

At daybreak the next morning, the party was attacked by Indians and all killed except Isaac Crabtree and Adam and Charles, the two slaves. Young Russell was shot through the hips and thus unable to escape. The Indians stabbed him with knives, and at each thrust he grabbed the blade with his hands. He was horribly mutilated. His hands were cut to pieces by the knife blades being drawn through them.

Sand Cave on the Kentucky side of Stone Mountain near Cumberland Gap.

Crabtree made good his escape and was the first to return to the settlement. Adam watched the butchery of his young master and others from a pile of driftwood. He became lost and wandered about for several days before reaching the settlement. Charles was taken captive, and after traveling about forty miles two of his captors quarreled over possession of him. The leader of the party, to settle the quarrel, tomahawked and killed him.

This tragedy temporarily ended the Kentucky settlement scheme, although Boone had wanted to go on in spite of the Indian hostilities. The party returned to Castlewood, where Boone served as a captain in the defense of the Clinch and Holston River frontier during the war which followed.

The final push to settle beyond Cumberland Gap began in 1775 when Boone and thirty ax men in the employment of Richard Henderson's Transylvania Company started cutting the Wilderness Road.

—Retold from Robert M. Addington, ***History of Scott County, Virginia***. *1932.*

Matthew Gray's Turkey Hunt

The legendary Benge, also called Captain Bench in some accounts, was a redheaded Indian war chief. He was a shrewd and fierce adversary who terrorized early settlers along the Clinch and Holston rivers. He belonged to the Chickamauga faction of the Cherokee, but also moved freely among the Shawnee whose warriors joined his raids on the thinly settled valleys. He was a contemporary of the notable war chiefs Dragging Canoe of the Cherokee and Logan of the Mingo. A bounty was offered to anyone brave enough to bring in his scalp.

In the spring of 1777 a war party led by the renegade war chief Benge and a white man named Hargus, accused of being a fugitive from crimes and debts in the colonies, and possibly a British agent agitating against the Americans, came down Stoney Creek into the Clinch valley. They had crossed the mountains somewhere around High Knob and approached Fort Blackmore (also known as Bluegrass Fort) near Osborn's Ford. The war party crossed the river and came up in the rear of a high cliff, nearly opposite the fort site. The raiders posted a lookout in a high cedar tree atop the cliff while the others concealed themselves below to ambush anyone passing. The lookout gobbled like a wild turkey to communicate with his confederates below and to lure unsuspecting settlers.

This imitation was so well executed it would have been successful but for the warnings of an old Indian fighter present by the name of Matthew Gray. Hearing what they supposed to be a turkey, and desiring him for breakfast, some of the younger members of the company proposed to go up the cliff and shoot him, but Gray told them if they wanted to keep their scalps on their heads they had better let that turkey alone, and if they would follow his directions he would give them an Indian for breakfast.

Having promised to obey his instructions, he took several of them with him to a branch which he knew to be in full view of the Indians. He told them to wash and dabble in the stream to divert the attention of the enemy for half an hour, while he went to look for the turkey, which still continued to gobble at short intervals. Gray, having borrowed an extra rifle from David Cox, crouched below the bank of the stream and in this manner followed its course to where it emptied into the river, half a mile below at a place known as Shallow Shoals. Here he took to the timber, eluding the vigilance of the Indians by getting in their rear. He crept cautiously up the ridge, guided by the gobbling of the Indian in the top of the cedar on the cliff. Getting to within about seventy-five yards of the tree, and waiting until his turkeyship had finished an extra big gobble, he drew a bead upon him and put a ball in his head.

Then commenced a race for life. Gray had played a desperate game, and nothing but his fleetness and his knowledge of savage craft could save him. He knew that the Indians in ambush would go to their companion on hearing the report of the rifle, and that they were not more than two hundred yards away. He did his best running and dodging, but they were so close upon him that he would have been captured or killed, had not the men of the fort rushed out to his rescue.

—*Retold from Robert M. Addington,*
***History of Scott County, Virginia**, 1932.*

Stoney Creek leads to the area of Fort Blackmore, Virginia, viewed from the lower slopes of High Knob.

Everything here assumes a dignity and splendor I have never seen in any other part of the world. Here an eternal verdure reigns and the brilliant sun piercing through the azure heavens produces in this prolific soil an early maturity truly astonishing.... Soft zephyrs gently breathe on sweets and the inhaled air gives a voluptuous glow of health and vigor that seems to ravish the intoxicated senses.... Everything here gives delight, and we feel a glow of gratitude for what an all-bountiful Creator has bestowed upon us.

—Charles McKnight,
Our Western Border, 1876.

The Miraculous Escape of Fannie Dickenson Scott

On June 20, 1785, about twenty Shawnee warriors, led by Benge, attacked the Archibald and Fannie Scott home at the head of Wallens Creek in Scott County, Virginia. Archibald and their five children were killed and Mrs. Scott taken captive. The party

Breaks Interstate Park on the Virginia/Kentucky border.

then headed north toward their villages beyond the Ohio. En route, while the others hunted, she was left in the charge of a single brave, who was to have her for a wife when they reached Miami. But he went to sleep and she escaped. She waded up a small stream to cover her tracks and hid in a canebrake. She wandered for weeks in the Cumberland Gap area, living on roots and berries. She was nearly recaptured on one occasion but crawled into a hollow sycamore to elude those hunting for her.

Slowly she traveled the forest paths toward her home but became disoriented in the deep wilderness. On reaching a fork in the path, she didn't know which way to turn, but finally decided to take the most traveled. But on setting out, a bird flew past her, touched her shoulder, and lighted in the other path. She kept on, however, but only got a few steps when the bird repeated the action. She took this as a sign that the other path must be the correct one and that the bird was the spirit of one of her murdered children come to guide her through the wilderness. The path pointed out by the bird led her through Pound Gap and on to Castlewood, where many of her relatives still live.

Fannie later married Thomas Johnson, for which Johnson County, Tennessee, is named. She lived to an old age and is buried at the base of Clinch Mountain near Hayter's Gap, Russell County, Virginia.

—Retold from Lewis Preston Summers,
***The History of Southwest Virginia**, 1903.*

Fall colors in the Appalachian hardwood forest of Clinch Mountain, Jefferson National Forest, of Southwest Virginia, near Mendota.

Benge's Last Raid

Peter Livingston was the owner of a large estate with slaves in Mendota, Virginia. This account, as recorded by Summers, was given by his wife, Elizabeth, in a deposition dated April 6, 1794, concerning her capture:

"About 10 o'clock in the morning, as I was sitting in my house, the fierceness of the dog's barking alarmed me. **I looked out and saw seven Indians approaching the house, armed and painted in a frightful manner. No person was then within, but a child of ten years old, and another of two, and my sucking infant. My husband and his brother Henry had just before walked out to a barn at some distance in the**

field. My sister-in-law, Susanna, was with the remaining children in an out-house. Old Mrs. Livingston was in the garden. I immediately shut and fastened the door; they (the Indians) came furiously up, and tried to burst it open, demanding of me several times to open the door, which I refused. They then fired two guns; one ball pierced through the door, but did me no damage. I then thought of my husband's rifle, took it down but it being double triggered, I was at a loss; at length I fired through the door, but it not being well aimed I did no execution; however the Indians retired from that place and soon after that an old adjoining house was on fire, and I and my children suffering much from the smoke. I opened the door and an Indian immediately advanced and took me prisoner, together with the two children. I then discovered that they had my remaining children in their possession, my sister Sukey, a wench with her young child, a negro man of Edward Callihan's and a negro boy of our own about eight years old....

"We were all hurried a short distance, where the Indians were very busy, dividing and putting up in packs for each to carry his part of the booty taken. I observed them careless about the children, and most of the Indians being some distance off in front, I called with a low voice to my eldest daughter, gave her my youngest child, and told them all to run towards neighbor John Russell's.

"They, with reluctance, left me, sometimes halting, sometimes looking back.... The two Indians in the rear either did not notice this scene, or they were willing the children might run back.

"That evening the Indians crossed Clinch Mountain and went as far as Copper creek, distant about eight miles.

"April 7th, set out early in the morning, crossed Clinch river...then steered northwardly towards the head of Stoney creek.... This day's journey was about twenty miles.

"April 8th....traveled five or six miles and camped near the foot of Powell's mountain. This day Benge, the Indian chief, became more pleasant, and spoke freely to the prisoners. He told them he was about to carry them to the Cherokee towns. That in his route in the wilderness was his brother with two other Indians hunting, so that he might have provision when he returned. That at his camp were several white prisoners taken from Kentucky, with horses and saddles to carry them to the towns.... He frequently enquired who had negroes, and threatened he would have them all off the North Holston. He said all the Chickamogga towns were for war, and would soon be very troublesome to the white folks.

"This day two of the party were sent by Benge ahead to hunt.

"April 9th. After travelling about five miles, which was over Powell's mountain, and near the foot of the Stone mountain, a party of thirteen men under command of Lieutenant Vincent Hobbs, of the militia of Lee County, met the enemy in front, attacked and killed Benge the first fire, I being at that time some distance off in the rear. The Indian who was my guard at first halted on hearing the firing. He then ordered me to run, which I performed slowly. He attempted to strike me in the head with the tomahawk, which I defended as well as I could with my arm. By this time two of our people came in view, which encouraged me to struggle all I could. The Indian making an effort at this instant pushed me backward, and I fell over a log, at the same time aiming a violent blow at my head, which in part spent its force on me and laid me for dead. The first thing I afterwards remembered was my good friends around me, giving me all the assistance in their power for my relief. They told me I was senseless for about an hour.

"Certified this 15th day of April, 1794.
"A CAMPBELL."

Lieutenant Hobbs and his men had been able to overtake the war party by taking a more direct route to Big Stone Gap and had prepared an ambush for Benge.

Chief Logan and Samuel Porter

On September 23, 1774, John Logan (a war chief of the Mingo) and a war party appeared before Fort Blackmore, one of forts then under command of Daniel Boone. They captured two slaves and numerous horses and cattle and paraded the captured slaves back and forth in view of the fort for a while. Then they proceeded to the Kings Mill area (today's Kingsport, Tennessee) where Logan killed a family named Roberts, except for a young boy who was captured. Here he left a war club and a letter written in gunpowder ink, challenging all the whites to fight him.

Logan's family had been brutally murdered by a Colonel Cresap while he was at peace. From that time he claimed that he had two souls, one good and one bad, and to avenge the deaths of his kin came under the dominion of his bad soul. His levy of death fell on the thinly settled valleys of East Tennessee and Southwest Virginia.

Peace came later that year, after the defeat of the French and Indians at Point Pleasant, but Chief Logan

Winter along Little Stoney Creek, near Dungannon, Virginia.

was not among those at the peace conference. When Governor Dunmore noticed his absence, he sent for him. Logan replied that he was a warrior, not a peacemaker, and sent his famous reply:

"I appeal to any white man to say if ever he entered Logan's cabin hungry and he gave him not meat; if ever he came cold and naked and he clothed him not? During the course of the last long and bloody war, Logan remained idle in his camp, an advocate for peace. Such was my love for the whites that my countrymen pointed as I passed and said, 'Logan is the friend of the white man.' I had even thought to have lived with you, but for the injuries of one man. Colonel Cresap, the last spring, in cold blood and unprovoked, murdered all the relations of Logan not even sparing my women and children. There runs not a drop of my blood in the veins of any living creature. This called on me for revenge. I have sought it. I have killed many. I have fully glutted my vengeance. For my country I rejoice at the beams of peace; but do not harbor a thought that mine is the joy of fear. Logan never felt fear. He will not turn on his heel to save his life. Who is there to mourn for Logan? Not one."

Another story involving Logan and the pioneers

An American Beech tree in fall color stands at Double Arch in the Red River Geological Area of eastern Kentucky.

Samuel and Patrick Porter of the Rye Cove area of Southwest Virginia has a happier ending:

Patrick Porter, while serving under General Lewis, in some capacity or other, on the Ohio River, was approached one day by Chief Logan, who, with a smile, extended his hand to Porter, at the same time saying, "I know you. You are Patrick Porter. I want to be your friend. You don't know me. I am Capt. John Logan. Many times I could have killed you, but I loved you, and would not." He then made enquiry about his son, Samuel, but, at that moment, seeing Samuel coming toward them, he pointed and said, "Yonder he comes." When Samuel came up, he said to him. "I am Logan; and was your friend. Many times I could have killed you, but would not. You were too good a man. You guarded the women and children, which made me love you and your father." On being assured of their perpetual love and friendship, he then rehearsed several occurrences that had taken place in the vicinity of Porter's Fort. One of the incidents recalled was concerning a large, fine horse that was hitched to the fort gate. By some chance, the horse was left there a great while, night coming on in the meantime. Logan, who was skulking near the fort, had watched the horse with covetous eyes. Taking advantage of the darkness, he tried to steal him. Covering himself with a shock of top fodder, he began gradually to approach the horse. But just at the moment when he was nearly ready to lay hold of the horse, a child inside the fort fell out of the bed, and made such a noise that Logan, fearing discovery, dropped the fodder, and left. "Did you ever notice that shock of fodder?" asked Logan. "Yes," replied Samuel Porter. "The breaking of that child's arm saved your life, Logan; I was on guard at the fort gate that night, and observing the fodder moving toward me, cocked my gun and was in the very act of firing when you dropped the fodder and ran away. I was within twenty feet of you, with as good a gun as was ever fired." Logan replied that the Great Spirit did not let one friend kill another.

—*Cited by Robert M. Addington,*
History of Scott County, Virginia, *1932.*

Watauga Lake in Northeast Tennessee in light winter snow.

Voyage of the Donelson Party

Early in 1780, during a bitterly cold winter, a group of about 200 people led by John Donelson left the Holston Valley settlements with the intention of relocating on the Cumberland River. James Robertson and another party had preceded them overland, in the fall of 1779, to plant a crop, build forts, and prepare for the arrival of the others who would travel by water. The Donelson party, on the "Good Boat *Adventure*," included Robertson's family, the women

Winter's grip in the Wilburn Ridge area of the Grayson Highlands of Virginia.

Tennessee Rivers, Donelson's party was joined by another group led by John Blackmore (for which Fort Blackmore was named). Only part of the group made it to their destination to found Nashboro (today's Nashville). The ordeal of one family from the Clinch settlements, recorded in Donelson's journal beginning on March 9, 1780, follows:

Help Poor Jennings

Thursday, 9th. Jennings' boat is missing. We have now passed through the Whirl. The river widens, with a placid and gentle current, and all the company appear to be in safety except the family of Jonathan Jennings, whose boat ran on a large rock projection out from the northern shore and partly immersed in water immediately at the Whirl, where we were compelled to leave them, perhaps to be slaughtered by their merciless enemies. Continued to sail on that day and floated throughout the following night.

Friday, 10th. This morning about 4 o'clock we were surprised by the cries of "Help poor Jennings" at some distance in the rear. He had discovered us by our fires and came up in the most wretched condition. He states that as soon as the Indians discovered his situation they turned their whole attention to him and kept up a most galling fire at his boat. He ordered his wife, a son nearly grown, a young man who accompanied them, and his negro man and woman to throw all his goods into the river in order to lighten his boat for the purpose of getting her off, himself returning the Indians' fire as well as he could, being a good soldier and an excellent marksman. But before they had accomplished their object, his son, the young man, and the negro jumped out of the boat and left them. He thinks the young man and the negro were wounded before they left the boat. Mrs. Jennings, however, and the negro woman succeeded in unloading the boat, but chiefly by the exertions of Mrs. Jennings, who got out of the boat and shoved her off, but was near falling a victim to her own intrepidity on account of the boat starting so suddenly as soon as loosened from the rock. Upon examination, he appears to have made a wonderful escape, for his boat is pierced in

and children, and goods needed to establish the community. Their plan was to float down the Holston and Tennessee Rivers, then to push up the Mississippi and the Ohio to the Cumberland, then finally up the Cumberland to the fort on French Bluffs to be built by Robertson. It was an ambitious plan since they had only partial knowledge of the route and landmarks, and it proved to be an epic saga filled with small and large dramas, including births, deaths, Indian attacks, and hardship. En route, at the confluence of the Clinch and

Roger's Ridge/Pond Mountain area near the point where North Carolina, Tennessee, and Virginia meet.

numberless places with bullets. Their clothes were very much cut with bullets, especially Mrs. Jennings'.
                    —*Journal of John Donelson, 1779-1780.*

One of the passengers on Jennings' boat was his daughter, Mrs. Ephraim Peyton, who had given birth to a son the day before. She also jumped into the water to help push the boat off the rocks, and her child was killed in the confusion, probably by drowning. Jennings' son and his companions who had jumped from the boat were captured. The other young man, whose name is not known, was burned at the stake, but young Jennings was ransomed by the trader John Rogers. Jonathan Jennings unfortunately didn't fair as well in Nashboro—he was killed, scalped, and his body cut into pieces in an attack by Delaware Indians about three months later.

Route of the Appalachian Trail covered with snow, near the summit of Hump Mountain, North Carolina.

Era of the American Revolution

During the years just preceding the American Revolution a rush of pioneers crossed the mountains from the Virginia, Pennsylvania, and North Carolina colonies into the Hogohcegee region (an Indian name for land between the Blue Ridge and Cumberland mountains). Major immigration routes entered the great valley from the north, through Virginia, and were detailed by Thomas Walker and other travelers. Two main routes also crossed the Blue Ridge from western North Carolina. One led from the Yadkin Valley through present-

The view southward from Bradley Gap on Hump Mountain, along the Tennessee/North Carolina border.

day Boone to Trade, on the Tennessee border, then passed down either the Watauga Valley, to settlements along it and the Nolichucky River, or down Taylor's Valley to settlements along the Holston and Clinch Rivers. The other crossed from the Morganton area, through the Linville/Newland area, then over Yellow Mountain Gap or Iron Mountain Gap to the settlements.

Many of those risking the uncertainties of the frontier were involved in varied development schemes, such as the Transylvania Company, or were avoiding the political unrest of the coastal and piedmont areas. With a constant threat of Indian hostilities and farms and plantations to be carved out of the wilderness, the "Overmountain" settlements had plenty to keep them

A light snow carpets the highlands along the Tennessee/North Carolina border on Little Hump Mountain.

busy. Many of the "Gentlemen" (this was still an era dominated by the privileged classes) leaders of these communities had political ambitions and obligations, but most would probably have taken little active role in the rebellion across the mountain barrier if events had not drawn them into the conflict.

British strategy was to have the war fought by Americans under British officers, to instigate Indians in the backwater areas and, by picking off the weaker colonies first, erode support for the Patriot cause. East of the mountains, loyalties were divided; but the longer the conflict went on, the more sentiments shifted to the Patriot side. Colonel Patrick Ferguson found neighbors bitterly divided in their loyalties, and recruitment for his army was below expectations. He probably made matters worse through his own bluster and arrogance. Intending to keep the overmountain settlements neutral, he sent word that they had better stay where they were, or he would cross the mountains and string up their "banditti" leaders. Rather than pacifying the mountain settlements, the message was taken as a threat or dare, and an army was quickly assembled.

Whatever the "Overmountain Men" lacked in military discipline they made up for in marksmanship

View of the Blue Ridge Mountains from the Tennessee/North Carolina border, with the Black Mountains in the top background.

and experience in the woodlands. Many fighting tactics had been adopted from the Indians.

Teddy Roosevelt in his **Winning of the West** gave this description of the Overmountain Men:

Their fringed and tasseled hunting-shirts were girded in by bead-worked belts, and the trappings of their horses were stained red and yellow. On their heads they wore caps of coon-skin or mink-skin, with the tails hanging down, or else felt hats, in each of which was thrust a buck's tail or a sprig of evergreen. Every man carried a small bore rifle, a tomahawk and a scalping knife. A very few of the officers

had swords, and there was not a bayonet nor a tent in the army.

The Overmountain Men

On September 26, 1780, the Overmountain Men left Sycamore Shoals (Elizabethton, Tennessee). Their route was up Gap Creek and the Doe River watershed to Bright's Trace which led across Yellow Mountain Gap. The open balds near the gap appear much as the area did

Coneflowers and butterfly at Yellow Mountain Gap.

when they passed, except that an early light snow lay on the peaks that day. In the open fields and meadows below the gap, the soldiers gathered into units and paraded under their respective officers.

The country that they had passed through to this point cannot be excelled in romantic grandeur anywhere on earth. It was excellently watered, broken by high mountains and interspersed with beautiful valleys. A North Carolina historian, in speaking of this country, says: "If we were to meet an army with music and banners we would hardly notice it. Man and all his works and all his devices are sinking into insignificance. We feel that we are approaching nearer and nearer to the Almighty Architect. We feel in all things about us the presence of the great Creator. A sense of awe and reverence comes over us, and we expect to find in this stupendous temple we are approaching none but men of pure hearts and benignant minds. But, by degrees, as we clamber up the winding hill, the sensation of awe gives way, new scenes of beauty and grandeur open upon our ravished visions, and a multitude of emotions swell within our hearts. We are dazzled, bewildered and excited, we know not how nor why; our souls expand and swim through the immensity before and around us, and our beings seem merged into the infinite and glorious works of God. This is the country of the fairies; and here they have their shaded dells, their mock mountains and their green valleys, thrown into ten thousand shapes of beauty. But higher up are the Titian hills; and when we get among them we will find the difference between abodes of the giants and their elfin neighbors."

—Lewis Preston Summers
The History of Southwest Virginia 1746-1786, 1903.

Late summer wildflowers near Yellow Mountain Gap on the Tennessee/North Carolina border. These meadows appear today much as they did when the Overmountain Men passed this way.

But also, while on these highlands, two members of the expedition deserted to warn Ferguson of the coming army. From Yellow Mountain Gap the expedition traveled down Roaring Fork and the North Toe River, then up Grassy Creek, across Gillespie's Gap on the Blue Ridge, and on to Kings Mountain, along the North and South Carolina border. This proved to be a turning point in the American Revolution in the South. Here the loyalist troop was overwhelmed and Ferguson was killed.

Goldenrod beside the Overmountain Victory Trail with Grassy Ridge and the Roan Highlands in the background.

To be in keeping with my wayward wanderings in this Alpine wilderness, it now becomes my duty to speak of the Roan Mountain.... It derives its name from the circumstance that it is often covered with snow, and at such times is of a roan color.... It...has three prominent peaks, which are all entirely destitute of trees. The highest of them has a clearing containing several thousand acres, and the cattle and horses of the surrounding farmers resort to it in immense numbers, for the purpose of feeding upon the fine and luxuriant grass which grows there in great abundance.... That it commands an uninterrupted view of what appears to be the entire world, may be readily imagined. When I was there I observed no less than three thunder storms performing their uproarious feats in three several valleys, while the remaining portions of the lower world were enjoying a deep blue atmosphere.

—Charles Lanman,
Letters From the Alleghany Mountains, 1848.

A late summer shower crosses the Highlands of Roan in this view from Yellow Mountain, Tennessee/North Carolina.

Bee balm/Oswego tea (red) and wild bergamot (white) in bloom between Yellow and Little Hump Mountains.

The Origin of Medicine
A Seneca Legend

There once lived a great man whose name was Bloody Hand. His fame as a hunter was not less than his reputation as a bold and resolute war captain. Many tribes claimed him as their brave son.

Now Bloody Hand had great love for the birds of the air and the animals on the earth that eat flesh. When he killed a deer he would cut it up and call the great Crow and feed him; other times he would call the fox and his family to eat. But one day all the members of a war party, including Bloody Hand, were ambushed by the enemy and killed. His body was left naked in the forest and his scalp taken as a trophy by the enemy. The birds saw him killed and mutilated and held a council to mourn his death.

Finally someone at the wake said: "Let us try to bring him back to life. But before we can begin to resuscitate his body we must recover his scalp, which hangs before the door of the chief of the enemy who killed him." They set about making preparations and conjuring with their most powerful medicine, and sent Black Hawk to retrieve the scalp. Black Hawk, with his powerful beak, was able to break the cords that held the scalp. He secured and bore it in triumph to the council.

Then one among them said: "Let us first try our medicine to see whether it has retained its virtue or not. We must try first to bring to life that dead tree which lies there on the ground." These were, of course, birds of the elder time, not such as live now, and they were able to make the tree grow as well as corn and squash. Then they were ready to aid Bloody Hand.

The wolves and snakes attended the ceremony, along with other animals and birds of great magic. The birds sang and the rattlesnakes rattled; all present made music, everyone in his own way.

Although it was late in the year, soon the assembly saw that the trees and plants were coming to life and putting forth green leaves and waxen buds like the beginning of spring. Then the presiding chief said to stop singing since the medicine would now work. He sent the medicine into Bloody Hand's stomach by the tiny Chickadee while everyone else began to rub his body with the potion. They resumed their singing, and in two days they felt him beginning to become warm again; still they sang, until at last he was fully recovered.

Late summer wildflowers near Yellow Mountain Gap.

The remainder of the potion was given to Bloody Hand to take back to his village, and he was told, "We bestow this medicine on you and your people. Your people shall have it for their healing. If it so happens that one of them is injured by a fall, by a blow, or by an arrow shot, he must have recourse to this medicine. You must also from time to time strengthen and renew this medicine by giving a feast in its honor. When you make use of it, you must burn tobacco in our behalf and turn your thoughts toward us."

The powerful medicine of Bloody Hand, and the secret songs and formulas for its use, are still maintained by the wise people of the northern tribes.

—*Retold from Jeremiah Curtin and J.N.B. Hewitt,* Seneca Fiction, Legends and Myths, *1910-1911.*

A view of the Linville Gorge, named for the unfortunate William Linville who was killed and scalped in the area in 1766, near the head of the Bynum Bluff Trail.

A Miracle of Mountain Justice

Maude Minish Sutton, a writer for the *Greensboro Daily News* of North Carolina, had sprained her ankle while hiking the Bynum Bluff trail in Linville Gorge. She got a ride back to town with an old mountain man on a wagon and he told her this story:

"Vengeance is mine, I will repay, says the Lord God of Hosts," he quoted with...exultant satisfaction.... "I have seen the guilty brought to punishment. I have behelt the forces of the Almighty at work. Ef something mistreats you or one of your kin, jest pray and your enemy will be delivered up into your hands. I have saw a miracle worked to bring the guilty to jestice.

"Ef you live as long as I have, you'll see hit more'n once," he said. "I've seed a sight of fightin' and shootin' in my day. I've buried a sight of folks that had got shot, but I hain't never put any murdered man away and had him to rest good, till the man who shot him was reckoned with. Blood calls fur blood you know.

"One time I was sent fur to bury a feller who had been found dead by a still house over yon side the Roan. Hit's been some odd year ago. Twa'n't long after I was called to preach. Nobody knowed anything about how he got killed. As fur back as anybody had knowed him they wa'n't a peaceabler feller on that side. His daddy talked to me before we went to the meetin' house.

"'I want him to have a decent burin',' the old man told me. 'Course he hain't a-goin' to see no rest till I git the hound that done hit.' He'd been shot in the back and hadn't never knowed what hit him. The old man said he had cleaned up his gun. I preached a strong sermon over that thar boy. And I prayed a powerful prayer. I was mighty in prayer in them days. I told the Lord about how some scamp had stoled up to that still house under cover of the night and shot that thar pore boy in his back. I told how he was snatched off right in a second without no time to make his peace. Let the murderer suffer fur the sins he hadn't give the pore boy time to beg forgiveness fur, I asked Him. Let the boy's pappy find out who done hit. 'You promised us that you'd let us take an eye fur an eye and a tooth for a tooth.' I says, 'Let this boy's pappy put a hole between that murderer's shoulders right whar his pore boy was shot. Pint him out to us, oh Lord.' I says. 'Help us to do thy vengeance.' You could hear the amens fur a mile. After that thar prayer we opened up the coffin and let the crowd pass by one at a time and look at him. His pappy stood right by the head of the coffin all the time, and watched the folks pass....

"Towards the back of the meetin' house had set a big feller from over 'cross State Line hill. He got up and

Gray's Lily (red) in bloom on Yellow Mountain, part of the Roan Highlands in Tennessee/North Carolina.

started up to look at the corpse.… When he got up by the corpse and looked at hit, he made a sort of a moanin' noise and says, 'I done hit.' The old man said, 'I knowed hit,' and drawed his gun. I jumped over the stand and cotched his hand, so he couldn't kill in the meetin' house. He got him next day though, and the hole was in the same place in his back that the one in the boy's was. While all this was a-goin' on I hadn't looked at the corpse. When I did I came near a-drappin' in a fit too. He had on a snow white bleachin' shirt and they was a big spot of blood big as a sasser on hit right over his heart. His pappy told me that the spot come right where that thar killer looked at him. The Lord jest plain showed the sign so's the old man could kill him.…"

—*Maude Minish Sutton,*
The Feud Spirit, *1927.*

Catawba Rhododendron bloom on Highlands of Roan, Grassy Ridge bald in North Carolina.

Story of a British Loyalist

Whilst separation and independence were imposing theories, so fascinating to the wild and restless spirits who had founded and were build-

Rhododendron gardens with Blue Ridge Mountains in background, near Carver's Gap, Tennessee/North Carolina.

ing up a vast empire in the western world, advocating their bold measures with absorbing zeal and desperate earnestness, there was a minority, many of whom were staid and sturdy, honest in purpose and courageous in conviction, who regarded the movement as unwarranted, and fraught with immediate peril and ultimate ruin. Despite persuasion, remonstrance, threats, social ostracism and what seemed to them persecution, they held allegiance to the Crown as a paramount duty, and regarded the war that must inevitably follow, in its destruction of the flower of the new country, as a twin horror....

At the close of the Revolutionary War, these tories ("loyalists," as they called themselves) were universally execrated;...they were put in stocks, chained to the public pillories, cast into prison, and beggared by the confiscation of their property, "without benefit of clergy."...

In the perspective of this group of terrible

scenes, heartaches, desolation of homes and disruption of families that the "common cause of liberty" might not perish, stands out a tragedy which, while it is of itself a melancholy picture of misfortune, suffering, despair and absolute want, is yet luminous with courageous manhood and the transcendent glory and conquering heroism of a pure and noble womanhood.

The story appears in three terse entries of the court records of Jonesborough, Tennessee:

Novr Term 1780. Ordered that the Commissioners advertise and sell the property of James Crawford & Thomas Barker, they...being found and taken in Arms Against the State.

May Term 1782: John Sevier a Commissioner of Confiscated property for the year 1781, made return that he sold Two Slaves Confiscated of the estate of Thomas Barker at the price of thirty four Hundred pounds, and that he have the money ready to Return.

Aug. Term 1782. The Court Order that Mrs. Ann Barker wife of Thomas Barker who stands charged with joining the British & was taken at Kings Mountain a prisoner, by the Americans & after that his estate was Confiscated by the County Court of Washington— On her application in behalf of her Husband for Tryal by Jury

Late summer wildflowers on Grassy Ridge, North Carolina.

the same is Accordingly Granted.

...

Thomas Barker came to the Watauga country immediately preceding or just after the formal Declaration of Independence was made by the colonies.... He was a large, handsome man, over the average in intelligence. He brought with him a fair library for the times, the best of household and kitchen furniture, some slaves and plenty of live stock and farming utensils. His purpose was to acquire an immense estate in lands, which he was preparing to do when the Revolution broke out in earnest. He was a "tory" from the start, and did not attempt to conceal his views....

These views had been expressed by Barker to the court which afterward confiscated his property,...on a charge of "treason." Barker also stated to the court that it was not his desire to take sides in the struggle; that he preferred, if let alone, to remain with them and his wife and children, but that, if forced to participate on one side or the other, he should take up arms for the "mother coun-

Laurel Fork Falls, on the route of the Appalachian Trail, in the Cherokee National Forest of Northeast Tennessee.

Crested Dwarf Iris along lower Laurel Fork Creek in Carter County, Tennessee

try." ...Barker finally left his home and joined the British army. He was captured at King's Mountain by some of the very men who constituted the court to which he had so boldly expressed his views more than a year before. He had been made a captain, and, according to tradition, commanded a company of tories at the battle....

After the battle of King's Mountain, the Americans... started home with the prisoners, arms, etc., captured in the battle. On the way, about October 12 to 14, a court martial was held at a point called Bickerstaff's Old Field, in Rutherford county, North Carolina, and some thirty or more of the prisoners were sentenced to be hanged—some for desertion from the American army, others for horse-stealing, and still others for crimes and outrages perpetrated on the people who were supporting the "common cause of liberty."

Nine or ten of those thus sentenced were hanged. However, Barker was defiant facing his accusers and...**stood with a scowl upon his face, and, holding up his open hands, said quietly: "I am unarmed; you can kill me, but you can't scare me!"**

He added that, if they stood by

Rime ice coats trees on Beauty Spot, Unaka Mountain, Tennessee/North Carolina.

prison, where he had been kept for a little more than a year and ten months, when his noble wife appeared in court in person, and procured the order granting him a trial by jury, given above.

This August term, 1782, was one long talked of and remembered for more reasons than one.... Few, very few women would have gone in person before such a court, to demand that a tory be granted a trial by jury; but Mrs. Antoinette Barker, wife of Thomas Barker, walked into court, with two (possibly three) small children with her. Their appearance was sufficient to excite sympathy: their faces were pale and haggard, and their clothing, although neat, was patched and worn. Mrs. Barker was a woman of fine appearance…but, depicted in every line of her countenance, were the traces of mental anguish and physical suffering. …but she stood up in the presence of that court, in all the magnificence of superior woman-hood, and, with the vehement eloquence of despair, pleaded the cause of her husband. All that she said will never be known; some things that she said were handed down from generation to generation. She "used the Dec-laration of Independence on the court"; she denied that her husband was a traitor…[and added] that he was her husband, and a kind and good one, and the father of her little, innocent, helpless children; that they had taken all of his property and left his family paupers; that he was then in prison, and had been for nearly two years, in con-sequence of which his health was altogether gone; that she and her little ones were without a protector, and that her neighbors and former friends had almost wholly for-saken her.

…Barker was released on his own recognizance, and never tried. Ruined in fortune, ostracized by friends, broken in spirit and in health, he could not endure his changed condition in life. He died soon after his release from prison, and the brave, faithful, noble but broken-hearted wife speedily followed her husband to the grave, leaving two or three children, the oldest a boy of some five or six years.

—*John Allison,*
Dropped Stitches in Tennessee History, *1897.*

and permitted him to be hanged for crimes he was incapable of committing, then he was no judge of men. Barker and Crawford were saved from the ignominious death by their former neighbors.

Barker was brought back to Jonesboro and put in

Snow blankets the slopes of Unaka Mountain, overlooking the Iron Mountain Gap area of Tennessee/North Carolina. This was a major overmountain route during the American Revolution era, the probable path of Andrew Jackson into the western country, and of those joining the British cause in the Carolinas.

The Jackson and Avery Duel

In the spring of 1778 Andrew Jackson, recently admitted to the practice of law, headed west from Morganton, North Carolina, to seek his fortune. His first stop was in the frontier town of Jonesborough, Tennessee, where he is supposed to have ridden into town with flare, astride a race horse, pistols strapped across the

Winter on Unaka Mountain, Tennessee/North Carolina.

Waightstill Avery was the most prominent man and the leading lawyer in Western North Carolina when Andrew Jackson came to the bar. At that time, and indeed from the time of the organization of the first court west of the Blue Ridge, Avery had the most extensive practice of any lawyer attending the courts east or west of the mountains.... He led the bold spirits of his day in his patriotic county, and was a member of the convention in 1775, at Mecklenburg, that declared for independence.... Such is the...man with whom Jackson fought the duel at Jonesboro, which shows that Avery was no ordinary man....

The account of the duel between Jackson and Avery, as given me,...agrees in the following particulars with that given by others: Jackson and Avery were opposing counsel in a suit being tried in the afternoon; the case was going apparently against Jackson's view and client; Jackson was exerting himself in an effort to escape from authorities relied on by Avery; and the latter did ridicule severely some legal position taken by his opponent....

Avery's favorite authority was "Bacon's Abridgment." This he carried with him from court to court, and from the tavern to the court house and back.... The book was carefully wrapped up in a piece of buckskin, to preserve it from wear. Avery quoted from and referred to "Bacon's Abridgment"...and Jackson had ridiculed Avery's pet authority.... Avery, in his retort, grew sarcastic; he not only criticized legal positions taken by Jackson, but intimated pretty strongly that he did not know anything about the law of that case or of any other, and that he had much to learn before he would be justified in criticizing a law book written by anyone. This was enough to inflame Jackson, and it did. Jumping to his feet, he exclaimed: "I may not know as much law as there is in Bacon's Abridgment, but I know enough not to take illegal fees!" Avery at once turned on Jackson, and demanded fiercely to know whether he meant to

saddle, and leading a pack of foxhounds. He quickly gained the reputation of a man who loved wagering on horses, cock fights, and other sporting pursuits. According to John Allison, "He was recognized from the first as a man who 'would fight at the drop of a hat, and drop the hat himself.'" It is uncertain whether he fought one duel or two at Jonesborough, and the details of the Avery affair favor either Jackson or Avery, depending on the bias of the many histories which include it.

A fall view of the Tennessee/North Carolina mountains and Nolichucky River area from Beauty Spot on the Appalachian Trail. Many of Andrew Jackson's early exploits, such as a hotly contested horse race in Greasy Cove and duels at Jonesborough, took place within view of these crests.

charge him with taking illegal fees. Jackson answered, "I do, sir," and started to say more; but Avery, pointing and shaking his finger at his adversary, hissed through his teeth, "It's as false as hell!" whereupon Jackson immediately sat down, picked up a law book, tore a blank leaf from it, wrote a challenge, delivered it to Avery, bowed to him ceremoniously, and walked out of the court house."

During negotiations concerning weapons and other points of the duel it was apparently agreed that there had

Fall colors near Spivey Gap, Tennessee.

given—and Jackson and Avery both fired in the air, to the great gratification of their friends.

The two principals approached each other with extended hands. While holding his recent antagonist by the hand, Jackson said: "Col. Avery, I knew that, if I hit you and did not kill you immediately, the greatest comfort you could have in your last moments would be to have 'Bacon's Abridgment' near you; and so I had my friend bring it to the ground." Thereupon, Jackson's second unrolled the package in his hand, which was about the size of a law book, and out fell a piece of old, well-cured bacon!

—*John Allison,*
***Dropped Stitches in Tennessee History**, 1897.*

been a mistake concerning fees on Avery's part, but that Jackson had not intended to accuse him of corruption.

Difficulties that led to a challenge and its acceptance, in the olden times, were rarely ever adjusted before the combatants arrived on the field. The distinguished duellists followed the custom on this occasion; and, with their seconds and others who knew of the affair, went to the ground selected—the hill on the south side of Jonesboro.... The distance was measured off, the principals stationed and the word

The Lost State of Franklin

The short-lived state of Franklin was closer to a "State of Appalachia" than has existed since. The boundaries, proposed by Arthur Campbell of Southwest Virginia, included all the mountains and valleys from the crests of the Blue Ridge westward to eastern Kentucky and West Virginia, and from the New and Kanawha Rivers southward into northern Georgia and Alabama.

Franklin had a brief tenure. Faced with large debts and growing obligations west of the mountains following the American Revolution, North Carolina, with encouragement from the new American government, renounced its claims and responsibilities for all its western lands in 1784. This left no government in the ceded territories, since the federal government had not yet established procedures to administer the regions. In this void the State of Franklin, named for Benjamin Franklin, was established.

For a time the new government operated more as a separate nation, waging war with the Indians, conducting treaties, issuing currency, levying taxes, and passing laws. But North Carolina quickly reversed its ceding of its western territories. For a time, two governments claimed authority in the region. A factional war threatened, with at least one small battle occurring near today's Johnson City, Tennessee, between bands loyal to Franklin led by its Governor, John Sevier, and those loyal to North Carolina led by John Tipton. Three people were killed in the engagement, and Franklin had a brief advantage, but North Carolina had again established its control over the area by 1788. North Carolina again ceded its lands west of the Alleghenies in 1790, and the region was organized into the Southwest Territory under the United States government.

With its capital first at Jonesborough, then at Greeneville, the State of Franklin had existed less than four years, from late 1784 to early 1788.

A late summer view of Rock Creek Falls in the Unaka Mountain Wilderness of Northeast Tennessee.

Rhododendron petals and toadstools carpet the forest floor near Spivey Gap, North Carolina.

Davy Crockett Rides an Elk to Court

Thar war a little ditty that happent the fust time I war sot up for Kongress.... I war going to election and had my rifle with me, with my dog Tiger, with two bottles of white face in my pockets. When I got about 1/2 way thar, and war in the forrest, I seed a cattymount up in a tree, and I clum up to git a fare shot at the cretur, and told tiger to be on hand if he war wanted. I war got on to the nixt branch to the won that the varmint war on, when he jumped down on to the limb and lit close to my elbow with his mouth to my ear, as if he war going to whisper sumthin mity private. I thort I war a gone sucker, but jist at that minnit the limb cracked and snapped off. I didn't stop to see what becum of the cattymount, but I went down, and wood ha' gone into the mud, only thar war a beg elk under the tree, and I lit upon his hind parts, and he give a rankantankerous jump which slid me down betwixt his horns like a gal in sighed siddle, and then eh put in all he knew. I like to ha' got my branes nocked out by the branches, and the way he went thro the forrest war like a driving snow storm.—All the trees and rocks seemed to be running the tother way; and Tiger couldn't keep up with us, and his pesky noise only maid the cretur run faster. I held on upon my rifle [but] found it hard work to taik aim, bekase the cretur woodn't give me a chance. Howsever he soon begun to git out of the forrest, and then I war terribly ashamed for feer sum human wood see me, but I coodn't see them as every thing looked streeked as if the American flag war spred over all nature....

I railly thort this war the eend of my travels, but the pesky varmint wheeled about, and went hed fourmost out the door agin, and shot ahead on the jump, four miles further, till he cum to the little eend of the Little Fork of Great Skunk's Liver River. We went rite thro the mob for the poles war held ther, and every boddy pulled off their hats and gin 3 cheers for Krockett, and that made me wrathy, and graniverous as a parched corn; bekase they din't try to stop the varmint at all. But they all hurried out of the way, and bauled—Hurrah for Crokett! Won feller from down East sed he sposed that war the way that our candy-dates war un for Kongress. I spose the elk war so skeered that he din't no what he war about. But it helped my lection, for they all thort it war an invention of my own, for to gratify the public. The elk had only gone a small peace further when we past by a store whar I war in dett a few dollars, and it war kepp by a Yankee, and he thort I war running away from my creditors. So he razed a hue and cry arter me, and in a minnit the hole village of Apple Toddy Creek war razed. They skeered the elk fust won way and then the tother, and he swang about and jostled me so that it skraped all the skin off my hinder eend, and I begun to feer if I got a seat in Kongress it wouldn't be of no use to me. Howsever

Rhododendron bloom in midsummer beside the Appalachian Trail near Spivey Gap, North Carolina/Tennessee.

the court war settin at the time, and the people skeered the cretur of that it run that way, and as the court house door was open, it run rite in. As soon as the judge seed me, sez he, "Thar's Crockett now! We war jist wanting yer for a witness in this ere kase of the Widder Strapup. You've cum in the nick of time."

The lawyer that war pleeding agin the widder stared open his eyes, and sez he, "I bleeve it is the Nick o'time, for the devil must ha' brot him to spile my kase."

I jumped rite off the elk, and gin my evidence, and that saved the widder's property; so she took the elk under her protexion, and arter he war broke, she used to ride him to meetin.

—1841 Crockett Almanac,
Containing Adventures, Exploits, Sprees & Scrapes in the West,
& Life and Manners in the Backwoods.

The Hermit of Bald Mountain

Charles Lanman viewed Bald Mountain on a journey between Asheville and Burnsville, North Carolina, in June 1848, and recorded the legend of David Greer.

The Appalachian Trail passes through beds of Fringed Phacelia on the slope of Bald Mountain, Tennessee.

"…Bald Mountain, which, being one of the loftiest in this section of country, and particularly barren, presented a magnificent appearance. On the extreme summit of this mountain is a very large and an intensely cold spring of water, and in its immediate vicinity are a small cave and the ruins of a log cabin, which are associated with a singular being named David Greer, who once made this upper world his home. He first appeared in this country about fifty years ago; his native land, the story of his birth, and his early history, were alike unknown…."

Greer, it seems, was desperately in love with the daughter of a local farmer, but his suit was rejected by the maid, and strenuously opposed by all her friends. Soon she was betrothed to another; and Greer, forsaking the company of people, retreated to the above mentioned bald to live as a recluse.

He proclaimed himself the owner of the entire mountain and that all who came there had to submit to his code of laws. He enforced his decree with a reputation as a "wild man" and with rifle shots from the highlands. Some years later the authorities of the county seat sent a messenger to Greer and demanded a poll-tax of 75 cents. The hermit said he would take care of it on the next court-day, and his word was accepted. Instead, on the appointed day he came to town and pelted the courthouse windows with rocks and drove the lawyers, judges and clients all out of the village, and with rifle in hand returned to his mountain.

For some months after this event he amused himself by mutilating all the cattle which he happened to discover on what he called his domain, and it is said he was in the habit of trying the power of his rifle by shooting down upon the plantations of his neighbors. The crowning event of David Greer's life, however, consisted in his shooting to the ground in cold blood,

The domain of David Greer, Big Bald Mountain summit, along the Tennessee/North Carolina line.

and in broad daylight, a man named Higgins. The only excuse that he offered for committing this murder was that the deceased had been found hunting for deer on that portion of land which Greer claimed as his own. For this offense, Greer was brought to trial; but he was acquitted on the ground of insanity. This enraged Greer and he cursed against the "injustice of the laws." There were several attempts on his life after that, perhaps because Higgins is a common surname in this land of blood feuds. Then mysteriously, after living for 20 years on the mountain, he tired of the solitary life and moved to one of the towns on the Tennessee side of the mountain. It was not long until he was in trouble again.

Autumn leaves collect in a pool along the Phillip's Hollow Trail in the Cherokee National Forest of Northeast Tennessee.

Early snow and maple leaves.

Greer had gone to work in an iron forge. In a dispute with a fellow workman, named Tompkins, Greer threatened to shoot him. Tompkins' friends recommended that he take the law into his own hands, and he shot Greer through the heart as he walked along the road with rifle in hand. Public opinion was on Thompkins' side, and he

was never summoned to account for the defensive murder he had committed.

—*Retold from*
Charles Lanman,
Letters From the Alleghany
Mountains, *1848.*

Autumn leaves along Gentry Creek in Johnson County, Tennessee.

Summer rain clouds cross the Blue Ridge Mountains in this view from Craggy Gardens, North Carolina.

For many a league to the southward clouds covered all the valleys in billows of white, from which rose a hundred mountain tops, like islands in a tropic ocean. My fancy sailed among and beyond them, beyond the horizon's rim, even unto those far seas that I had sailed in my youth, to the old times and the old friends that I should never see again.
—Horace Kephart, **Our Southern Highlanders**, 1913.

Ferns and asters on the Craggy Gardens Trail in North Carolina.

September 18, 1887:
    ...Oh, these forest gardens of our Father! What perfection, what divinity, in their architecture! What simplicity and mysterious complexity of detail! Who shall read the teaching of the sylvan pages, the glad brotherhood of rills that sing in the valleys, and all the happy creatures that dwell in them under the tender keeping of a Father's care?

—John Muir,
A Thousand-Mile Walk to the Gulf,
1887.

I enjoyed two mountain landscapes, which were supremely beautiful and imposing. The first was a northern view of Black Mountain from the margin of the South Toe river, and all its cliffs, defiles, ravines, and peaks seemed as light, dreamlike, and airy as the clear blue world in which they floated. The stupendous pile appeared to have risen from the earth with all its glories in their prime, as if to join the newly-risen sun in his passage across the heavens.... The only sounds that fell upon my ear, as I gazed upon this scene, were the murmurings of a distant water-fall, and the hum of insect wings.

—Charles Lanman,
Letters From the Alleghany Mountains, 1848.

Roaring Fork Falls, Black Mountains, North Carolina.

The South Toe River, Western North Carolina, Pisgah National Forest.

Linville Falls framed by blooming rhododendron, North Carolina.

I come now to speak of the Lindville Falls, which are situated on the Lindville river, a tributary of the beautiful Catawba. They are literally embosomed among mountains, and long before seeing them do you hear their musical roar. The scenery about them is as wild as it was a hundred years ago —not even a pathway has yet been made to guide the tourist into the stupendous gorge where they reign supreme.... [It is] an easy matter to imagine it a monument erected by Nature to celebrate her own creative power.

With a liberal hand, indeed, has she planted her forest trees in every imaginable place; but with a view of even surpassing herself, she has filled the gorge with a variety of caverns, which astonish the beholder, and almost cause him to dread an attack from a brotherhood of spirits.

—Charles Lanman,
**Letters From the
Alleghany Mountains,**
1848.

The sky is painted with the colors of dawn, looking along the Blue Ridge Crest toward the Black Mountains of North Carolina.

Mount Mitchell Area: Black Mountains

"Life in its becoming is always shedding death," stated Joseph Campbell. His books explore the universal themes of religion and myth, the taking and giving of life, and the spiritual journey of humanity. "Anyone who has had an experience of mystery knows that there is a dimension of the universe that is not that which is available to his senses. There is a pertinent saying in one of the Upanishads: 'When before the beauty of a sunset or of a mountain you pause and exclaim, "Ah", you are participating in divinity.' Such a moment of participation involves a realization of the wonder and sheer beauty of existence."

Standing atop the high ridges of the Black Mountains, which include the highest peaks in the Appalachian chain, the vastness of God's natural creation is displayed in rolling waves of tree-covered highlands. But the summer lushness of green and growing things is frequently broken by bleached white skeletons of dead and dying trees, and their numbers increase with the altitude, until the crowns appear as ghost forests.

Official explanations of the stark contrast between the thriving vegetation of the lower elevations and the devastation on the peaks are inconclusive.

The role of acid precipitation (which is heavier in the cooling of higher elevations) in the increased vulnerability of highland trees to other stresses is difficult to prove beyond debate. Studies continue.

Meanwhile, the trees on all the higher summits in the Appalachian Mountains are afflicted to some extent by unusually high mortality and slow growth rates. Rising soil and stream acidity has been documented, and its detrimental effects established. But in the bureaucratic and political arenas of polished marble and granite, this alarming decline in the natural environment is far away. More immediate concerns revolve around cost verse benefits relationships.

No one is blameless. This killing of the natural world is required to bring to life a throw-a-way, mass culture dependent on cheap electrical power, internal combustion engines, uncontrolled industrial emissions, fly-by-night real estate developments, and disposable everything. Some of these excesses could be reduced through conservation, recycling, and mass awareness.

The idea of the interdependence of all life is not a prevailing viewpoint. Contempt for nature, evidenced by thrown away beer cans and trash, even in the most remote corners of our forest, is an attitude that has developed through generations. In western religious traditions, our animal nature and the natural world is regarded as our darker side, symbolized in the expulsion of Adam and Eve from the Garden of Eden, to be controlled and subordi-

Basin below Crabtree Falls, Pisgah National Forest, North Carolina.

nated. On the plus side, this ideology of nature, the enemy to be conquered, has resulted in an aggressive technology and unequaled standards of living. But evidence is building that if accommodations aren't made to sustain the conquered earth, before every tree is cut and every free-flowing stream dammed, we will destroy ourselves in the process.

Walking softly through the high forest of Appalachia, we can reach out and touch the radiant energy of surrounding life, a radiance that shines from trees, ferns, wildflowers, deer, bear, insects, birds, and even the stone itself, a light that shines through all things. Where does this transcendent energy come from, or go? If the Supreme Being had no hand in the creation of this world, as philosophers have asked for centuries, then why is there something, rather than nothing. Intangible concepts of soul, spirit, compassion, and love do not fit easily into evolving technologies. Ancient concepts that integrate people into the greater cosmos may prove to be more than primitive superstition. The spiritual nature of mankind, the poetic identity with all existence, and the mystery of the sacred spark of life, so richly felt in ancient mythology and shed somewhere on the road to creature comforts, are missing in agnostic realizations. The spiri-

A summer storm crosses the Blue Ridge crest, viewed from Mount Craig in the Black Mountains of North Carolina.

tual quest may be felt in all things of beauty, man-made as well as natural. It is that fleeting sensation of awe before a great work of art, the exhilaration from a concert or drama, the vitality and excitement of a moment in sports, the reverence before an ancient building or monument; it is an intangible feeling of humility and brief awareness that we are alive and part of all life, that this is IT. This is what makes the rest, both sorrow filled and dry blandness, bearable. It is the tingling sensation we felt often in the discoveries of youth, but an awareness hard to savor or hang on

to, without the intrusion of mundane thoughts of everyday survival, in adulthood.

There is a quieter, lyrical center along forested paths, nearer original creation, where recently mechanized humanity seems less significant amid the profusion of life that is the legacy of the sacred land. All the societies of man are but one slender branch of the ancient tree of life, clinging above the gaping abyss of infinite time. In the deep wood there is present an abiding sense of the great mystery from which we sprang, an enhanced sensitivity to

Bluets and galax on the slope of Mount Mitchell, highest peak in the eastern United States, North Carolina.

the everlasting world, our journey in it, and responsibility to it. The Middle East has been proclaimed the Holy Land by Christianity, Judaism, and Islam, but the remaining, unspoiled highlands of Appalachia are also a holy land, worthy of deep reverence and protection.

Viewing the sublime beauty of rolling mountains from the top of Mount Mitchell leaves little doubt that at least a part of Eden remains to be cherished. Campbell summarizes the earth-celebrating traditions by citing the idea of Buddha consciousness: "...an immanent, luminous consciousness that informs all things and all lives," and in a passage from the **Gnostic Gospel According to St. Thomas**, "The Kingdom of the Father is spread upon the earth and men do not see it."

The Nature of Life After Death

William Byrd cited the beliefs of a Saponi Indian named Bearskin. His tribe lived in the Staunton River region during the colonial era.

He believ'd that after death both good and bad people are conducted by a strong guard into a great road, in which departed souls travel together for some time, till at a certain distance this road forks into two paths, the one extremely levil, and the other stony and mountainous. Here the good are parted from the bad by a flash of lightning, the first being hurry'd away to the right, the other to the left. The right hand road leads to a charming warm country, where the spring is everlasting, and every month is May; and as the year is always in its youth, so are the people, and particularly the women are bright as stars, and never scold. That in this happy climate there are deer, turkeys, elks, and buffaloes innumerable, perpetually fat and gentle, while the trees are loaded with delicious fruit quite throughout the four seasons. That the soil brings forth corn spontaneously, without the curse of labour, and so very

Dogwoods form the understory of Appalachian hardwoods on the slopes of Mount Mitchell, North Carolina.

Dead and dying Fraser fir trees along the skyline of Mount Mitchell, North Carolina.

wholesome, that none who have the happiness to eat of it are ever sick, grow old, or dy. Near the entrance into this blessed land sits a venerable old man on a mat richly woven, who examines strictly all that are brought before him, and if they have behav'd well, the guards are order'd to open the crystal gate, and let them enter into the land of delights.

The left hand path is very rugged and uneven, leading to a dark and barren country, where it is always winter. The ground is the whole year round cover'd with snow, and nothing is to be seen on the trees but icicles. All the people are hungry, yet have not a morsel of anything to eat.... Here all the women are old and ugly, having claws like a panther, with

Early fall ferns and asters on Max Patch Mountain, Tennessee/North Carolina.

A squirrel sits atop a marker for the Appalachian Trail on the open balds of Max Patch, in the Pisgah National Forest of North Carolina.

which they fly upon the men that slight their passion. For it seems these haggard old furies are intolerably fond, and expect a vast deal of cherishing. They talk too much, and exceedingly shrill.... At the end of this path sits a dreadful old woman on a monstrous toad-stool, whose head is cover'd with rattle-snakes instead of tresses, with glaring white eyes, that strike a terror unspeakable into all that behold her. This hag pronounces sentence of woe upon all the miserable wretches that hold up their hands at her tri-

bunal.... Here, after they have been tormented a certain number of years...they are again driven back into this world, to try if they will mend their manners, and merit a place the next time in the regions of bliss.

—William Byrd,
The History of the Dividing Line Between Virginia and North Carolina, as run in 1728-29, and A Journey to the Land of Eden.

Early fall asters, ferns, and goldenrod line a path on Max Patch Mountain in western North Carolina.

Sassafras bushes form the understory along the Chimney Tops Trail of the Cherokee National Forest, overlooking Weaver's Bend on the French Broad River.

In every order of nature, we perceive a variety of qualities distributed amongst individuals, designed for different purposes and uses, yet it appears evident, that the great Author has impartially distributed his favours to his creatures, so that the attributes of each one seem to be of sufficient importance to manifest the divine and inimitable workmanship...though none of these most useful tribes are conspicuous for stateliness, figure or splendor, yet their valuable qualities and virtues, excite love, gratitude and adoration to the great Creator, who was pleased to endow them with such eminent qualities, and reveal them to us for our sustenance, amusement and delight.

—William Bartram, **The Travels of William Bartram**, 1775.

Cullasaja Gorge in the Nantahala Mountains of North Carolina.

Winesprings Bald along the William Bartram Trail in western North Carolina. This foot path is approximately the route followed by the botanist into Appalachia in 1775.

In the spring of 1775 William Bartram traveled across the Blue Ridge crest identifying and drawing much of the region's plant life. His route across Waya Bald and Winespring Bald to the Nantahala River is commemorated in a hiker trail through the Nantahala National Forest. Much of the path appears today as he would have seen it around May 24 and 25, 1775.

Perhaps there is not any part of creation, within the reach of our observations, which exhibits a more glorious display of the Almighty hand, than the vegetable world. Such a variety of pleasing scenes, ever changing, throughout the seasons, arising from various causes and assigned each to the purpose and use determined.

—William Bartram,
The Travels of William Bartram, 1775.

The Lost Paradise

James Mooney left an invaluable documentation of American Indian ethnology. Among his works are: *Myths and Legends of the Cherokee, Sacred Formulas of the Cherokee, The Siouan Tribes of the East,* and *The Ghost-Dance Religion.* In his introduction to the stories of Pontiac and Tecumseh, he offered the following perspective on their struggles:

The wise men tell us that the world is growing happier—that we live longer than did our fathers, have more of comfort and less of toil, fewer wars and discords, and higher hopes and aspirations. So say the wise men; but deep in our own hearts we know they are wrong. For were not we, too, born in Arcadia, and have we not—each one of us—in that May of life when the world was young, started out lightly and airily along the path that led through green meadows to the blue mountains on the distant horizon, beyond which lay the great world we were to conquer? And though others dropped behind, have we not gone on through morning brightness and noonday heat, with eyes always steadily forward, until the fresh grass began to be parched and withered, and the way grew hard and stony, and the blue mountains resolved into gray rocks and thorny cliffs? And when at last we reached the toilsome summits, we found the glory that had lured us onward was only the sunset glow that fades into darkness while we look, and leaves us at the very goal to sink down, tired in body and sick at heart, with strength and courage gone, to close our eyes and dream again, not of the fame and fortune that were to be ours, but only of the old-time happiness that we have left so far behind.

As with men, so it is with nations. The lost paradise is the world's dreamland of youth. What tribe or people has not had its golden age, before Pandora's box was loosed, when women were nymphs and dryads and men were gods and heroes? And when the race lies crushed and groaning beneath an alien yoke, how natural is the dream of a redeemer, an Arthur, who shall return from exile or awake from some long sleep to drive out the usurper and win back for his people what they have lost. The hope becomes a faith and the faith becomes the creed of the priests and prophets, until the hero is a god and the dream a religion, looking to some great miracle of nature for its culmination and accomplishment. The doctrines of the Hindu avatar, the Hebrew Messiah, the Christian millennium, and the Hesunanin of the Indian Ghost dance are essentially the same, and have their origin in a hope and longing common to all humanity.

—James Mooney,
The Ghost-Dance Religion, *accompanying paper of the*
Fourteenth Annual Report of the
Bureau of American Ethnology to the
Secretary of the Smithsonian Institution, *1896.*

The Delaware Prophet and the Quest of Pontiac

The Delaware tribe ranged throughout the eastern woodlands, from the coast to at least the Cumberland, Ohio, and Great Lakes regions. They were respectfully referred to by the Cherokee as "Grandfather." In 1762 a prophet appeared among them who preached a union of all the red tribes and a return to the old Indian life.

According to the prophet's story, as recorded by Mooney:

Being anxious to know the "Master of Life," he determined…to undertake a journey to the spirit world. Ignorant of the way, and not knowing any person who…could direct him, he performed a mystic rite in the hope of receiving some light as to the course he should pursue. He fell into a deep sleep, in which he dreamed that it was only necessary to begin his journey and that by continuing to walk forward he would at last arrive at his destination.

Early the next morning, taking his gun, ammunition, and kettle, he started off, firmly convinced that by pressing onward without discouragement he should accomplish his object. Day after day he proceeded without incident, until at sunset of the eighth day, while preparing to encamp for the night by the side of a small stream in a little opening in the forest, he noticed, running out from the edge of the prairie, three wide and well-trodden paths. Wondering somewhat that they should be there, he finished his temporary lodging and, lighting a fire, began to prepare his supper. While thus engaged, he observed with astonishment that the paths became more distinct as the night grew darker…. It seemed to him that one of these roads must lead to the place of which he was in search, and he determined, therefore, to remain where he was until morning and then take one of the three and follow it to the end. Accordingly, the next morning, after a hasty meal, he left his encampment, and, burning with the ardor of discovery,…he

explored the paths. There were great fires at the end of the first two that turned him back, and at the end of the third, smallest lane he came to the foot of a sheer mountain wall that blocked his passage.

He was about to give way to disappointment, when, looking up, he saw seated a short distance up the mountain a woman of bright beauty and clad in snow-white garments, who addressed him in his own language, telling him that on the summit of the mountain was the abode of the Master of Life, whom he had journeyed so far to meet. "But to reach it," said she, "you must leave all your cumbersome dress and equipments at the foot, then go and wash in the river which I show you, and afterward ascend the mountain….

After climbing the mountain, using only his left hand and foot, as his guide instructed, he reached an enchanted land. After admiring the beauty of everything about him, he was then conducted into the presence of the Master of Life who commanded him to exhort his people to cease from drunkenness, wars, polygamy, and the medicine song, and continued:

"The land on which you are, I have made for you, not for others…. Again become good and do my will and I will send animals for your sustenance…. [And with those who trouble you] drive them away; wage war against them; I love them not; they know me not…. Send them back to the lands I have made for them. Let them remain there."

The prophet then spread his message to all the tribes who would listen, along with the special prayers that he said came from the Master of Life. He told the Indians to discard everything that had come from the whites and return to the old ways, including bow and arrows and making fire with rubbing sticks, and for all the tribes to unite against the whites.

This message was taken up by the celebrated chief,

Serviceberry tree blooms above the South Fork of the Cumberland River, along the John Muir Trail, Big South Fork National Recreation Area, Tennessee/Kentucky.

Pontiac (or Little Turtle), who sought to form a grand confederacy of all the tribes to oppose the English.

Pontiac organized simultaneous, crushing attacks at British posts scattered throughout the 500 miles of wilderness from Pittsburgh to the straits of Mackinaw.

He was finally defeated after twenty years of constant war, cut down by a hired assassin of his own race. But the idea of Indian unity was then revived by the Shawnee leader Tecumseh.

Tecumseh: Great Leader of the Shawnee and His Brother the Prophet

Now arose among the Shawano another prophet to point out to his people the "open door" leading to happiness. In November, 1805, a young man named Laulewasikaw, then hardly more than 30 years of age, called around him his tribesmen and their allies at their ancient capital of Wapakoneta, within the present limits of Ohio, and there announced himself as the bearer of a new revelation from the Master of Life, who had taken pity on his red children and wished to save them from the threatened destruction. He declared that he had been taken up to the spirit world and had been permitted to lift the veil of the past and the future—had seen the misery of evil doers and learned the happiness that awaited those who followed the precepts of the Indian god....

He set out the need to renounce the white influences and said that the Great Spirit would intervene on the side of the Indians if they would return to the old ways. His teachings spread to all the tribes. His followers destroyed their guns and other trade goods and even killed their cats.

Less flattering accounts of the prophet stated: "The prophet was noted for his stupidity and intoxication until his fiftieth year..." and that he had his detractors killed, including an old woman burned alive.

His word aroused an intense excitement among his hearers, and the impression deepened as the tidings of the new gospel were carried from camp to camp.

The prophet now changed his name to Tenskwatawa, "The open door," significant of the new mode of life which he had come to point out to this people, and fixed his headquarters at Greenville, Ohio....

By some means he had learned that an eclipse of the sun was to take place in the summer of 1806. As the time drew near, he called about him the scoffers and boldly announced that on a certain day he would prove to them his supernatural authority by causing the sun to become dark. When the day and hour arrived and the earth at midday was enveloped in the gloom of twilight, Tenskwatawa, standing in the midst of the terrified Indians, pointed to the sky and cried, "Did I not speak truth? See, the sun is dark!" There were no more doubters now. All proclaimed him a true prophet and the messenger of the Master of Life. His fame spread abroad and apostles began to carry his revelations to the remotest tribes.

A number of catastrophes were predicted to afflict the whites and Indian nonbelievers—among the Creeks and Cherokee, it was believed there would come a great hail storm which would destroy them. The believers were supposed to be saved from the storm by retreating to the high mountains of the Smokies. In the fall of 1811 many believers in the prophesies left all their properties in the lowlands and went to the mountains for haven but returned sheepishly when the storm did not occur.

Tecumseh was also considered a great mystic by his followers. He interpreted the new revelations and message to return to the old ways as a cause to unite all the Indian tribes and expel the whites, much as Pontiac had taught. These Indian aspirations were encouraged by the British, since another war with the Americans seemed inevitable.

Tecumtha, "The Meteor", was the son of a chief and the worthy scion of a warrior race. His tribe, the Shawano, made it their proud boast that they of all tribes had opposed the most determined resistance to the encroachments of the whites. His father had fallen under the bullets of the Virginians while leading his warriors at the bloody battle of Point Pleasant, in 1774. His eldest and dearest brother had lost his life in an attack on a southern frontier post, and

Moss and lichens surround a pine thicket along the John Muir Trail in the Big South Fork National Recreation Area, Tennessee/Kentucky.

another had been killed fighting by his side at Wayne's victory in 1794. What wonder that the young Tecumtha declared that his flesh crept at the sight of a white man.

Even so, he advocated the humane treatment of prisoners and induced the tribe to give up the practice of burning their captives. His name has also been rendered "The Shooting Star" and "The Panther Lying in Wait—or Crouching Lion" in various translations.

The Shawnee hunted from the Cumberland to the Susquehanna, and had formerly lived along the Savannah and Suwanee Rivers. At various times they had been allied with the Chickamauga faction of the Cherokee and had been under the protection of the Delaware. They had also been called the Gypsies of the Forest and were renowned for their conjuring and stealth.

It was Tecumseh's position that the boundary for Indian lands should be rolled back to the Ohio River and that the treaties they had signed were invalid since they were contracted under duress. They moved their headquarters to the western bank of the Wabash, just below the mouth of the Tippecanoe.

In the summer of 1811 Tecumseh went on a long visit to the southern tribes to enlist them into the Indian league he was forming. American troops took advantage of his being away by attacking and destroying the confederation's stronghold on the Wabash, discrediting the prophet and his teaching of spiritual protection for their followers at the same time.

On this trip Tecumseh went as far as Florida and engaged the Seminole for his confederacy. Then, retracing his steps into Alabama, he came to the ancient Creek town of Tukabachi, where, according to McKenney and Hall's History of the Indian Tribes of North America, the following occurred:

"He made his way to the lodge of the chief called the Big Warrior. He explained his object, delivered his war talk, presented a bundle of sticks, gave a piece of wampum and a war hatchet—all which the Big Warrior took—when Tecumthe', reading the spirit and intentions of the Big Warrior, looked him in the eye, and, pointing his finger toward his face, said: 'Your blood is white. You have taken my talk, and the sticks, and the wampum, and the hatchet, but you do not mean to fight. I know the reason. You do not believe the Great Spirit has sent me. You shall know. I leave Tuckhabatchee directly, and shall go straight to Detroit. When I arrive there, I will stamp on the ground with my foot and shake down every house in Tuckhabatchee.' So saying, he turned and left the Big Warrior in utter amazement at both his manner and his threat, and pursued his journey. The Indians were struck no less with his conduct than was the Big Warrior, and began to dread the arrival of the day when the threatened calamity would befall them. They met often and talked over this matter, and counted the days carefully to know the day when Tecumthe' would reach Detroit. The morning they had fixed upon as the day of his arrival at last came. A mighty rumbling was heard—the Indians all ran out of their houses—the earth began to shake; when at last, sure enough, every house in Tuckhabatchee was shaken down. The exclamation was in every mouth, 'Tecumthe' has got to Detroit!' The effect was electric. The message he had delivered to the Big Warrior was believed, and many of the Indians took their rifles and prepared for the war. The reader will not be surprised to learn that an earthquake had produced all this; but he will be, doubtless, that it should happen on the very day on which Tecumthe' arrived at Detroit, and in exact fulfillment of this threat. It was the famous earthquake of New Madrid on the Mississippi."

The Creek War with the Americans broke out in 1812. This led to the complete defeat of the Creeks at the Battle of Horseshoe Bend by the combined Cherokee and American armies under Andrew Jackson.

In the North, events went no better for the Indian cause. Tecumseh and his remaining force joined the British in Canada, where he had the rank of Brigadier General. The story of his last battle, as related by Drake in Life of Tecumseh and of his Brother the Prophet..., follows:

"The Indian leader had no hope of triumph in the issue. His sun had gone down, and he felt himself already standing in the shadow of death. He was done with life and desired only to close it, as became a warrior, striking a last blow against the hereditary enemy of his race. When he had posted his men, he called his chiefs about him and calmly said, 'Brother warriors, we are now about to enter into an engagement from which I shall never come out—my body will remain on the field of battle.' He then unbuckled his sword, and, placing it in the hands of one of them, said, 'When my son becomes a noted warrior and able to wield a sword, give this to him.' He then laid aside his British military dress and took his place in the line, clothed only in the ordinary deerskin hunting shirt.... Tecumtha died in this forty-fourth year."

—Cited by James Mooney,
The Ghost-Dance Religion, 1896.

South Fork of Cumberland River, along John Muir Trail, Big South Fork National Recreation Area, Tennessee/Kentucky.

September 12, 1887:

There is nothing more eloquent in Nature than a mountain stream.... Its banks are luxuriantly peopled with rare and lovely flowers and overarching trees, making one of Nature's coolest and most hospitable places. Every tree, every flower, every ripple and eddy of this lovely stream seemed solemnly to feel the presence of the great Creator. Lingered in this sanctuary a long time thanking the Lord with all my heart for his goodness in allowing me to enter and enjoy it.

—John Muir, **A Thousand-Mile Walk to the Gulf,** 1887.

Autumn reflections along the South Fork of the Cumberland River, Big South Fork National Recreation Area, Tennessee/Kentucky.

The Lost American Colony of Welsh Prince Madoc

Madoc was one of the younger sons of the last independent Prince of Wales, Owen Gwynned, in the 15th century. Madoc became sick of the fighting for control of the realm following the death of Owen and decided to find another place to live. He and his companions sailed west in three boats in search of new lands. They were supposed to have landed in the Mobile Bay area and established a small colony.

Madoc then returned to Wales with glowing descriptions of the lush, new lands he had discovered. He recruited 3,000 other immigrants and set sail to join the earlier colony. According to Welsh folklore, none of the colonists were ever heard from again. There is a tradition of a tribe of White Indians" in several of the

North Arch, with fall maple trees, in the Twin Arches area of the Big South Fork National Recreation Area, Tennessee/Kentucky.

Southern tribes' mythologies. According to these stories, the White Indians prospered for a while, but through wars with neighboring tribes they were pushed inland toward the Cumberland region and were eventually annihilated or dispersed into small communities. The Cherokee accounts state that the White Indians became more and more savage, until they were defeated by the Cherokee and forced to move west.

White Indians—or a tribe lighter than the others—were reported by early explorers as well, including the de Soto expedition.

Some early historians claimed there were Welsh words and phrases in the Tuscarora and Shawnee languages. White Indians were also reported by George Rogers Clark, Daniel Boone, John Sevier, and the Reverend Morgan Jones in the 1700s. Jones claimed he was captured by a band of Indians who were in the process of burning him at the stake when, in terror, he reverted to his native Gaelic language to address them. They released him and greeted him as a brother.

John James Audubon on the American Pigeon

John James Audubon, a native of France, immigrated to Louisville, Kentucky, in 1807. Following failed attempts at business as a storekeeper, sign painter, and tutor, he sold subscriptions for his **Ornithological Biography**, issued in three volumes, which brought him fame and fortune. The National Audubon Society bears his name.

His graphic descriptions of the migration and hunting of pigeons in Kentucky and the Ohio Valley are typical of scenes that took place throughout the region.

During the mid-1800s in Knoxville, Tennessee, the birds were traded by the ton for shipment to distant ports. The Smokies and Pigeon River areas were famed for their huge flocks, and as their population began to decline, even the trees at their nesting sites were cut to get at the birds and eggs. All that remains of the American passenger pigeon is its name.

The multitudes of Wild Pigeons in our woods are astonishing. Indeed, after having viewed them so often, and under so many circumstances, I even now feel inclined to pause, and assure myself that what I am going to relate is fact. Yet I have seen it all, and that too in the company of persons who, like myself, were struck with amazement.

In the autumn of 1813...I observed the Pigeons flying from north-east to south-west, in greater numbers than I thought I had ever seen them before, and feeling an inclination to count the flocks that might pass within the reach of my eye in one hour, I dismounted, seated myself on an eminence, and began to mark with my pencil, making a dot for every flock that passed. In a short time finding the task which I had undertaken impracticable, as the birds poured in countless multitudes, I rose, and counting the dots then put down, found that 163 had been made in twenty-one minutes. I traveled on, and still met more the farther I proceeded. The air was literally filled with Pigeons; the light of noon-day was obscured as by an eclipse....

Before sunset I reached Louisville, distant from Hardensburgh fifty-five miles. The Pigeons were still passing in undiminished numbers, and continued to do so for three days in succession. The banks of the Ohio were crowded with men and boys, incessantly shooting at the pilgrims, which there flew lower as they passed the river. Multitudes were thus destroyed. For a week or more, the population fed on no other flesh than that of Pigeons, and talked of nothing but Pigeons....

He then described a pigeon hunt:

One of these curious roosting-places, on the banks of the Green River in Kentucky, I repeatedly visited. It was, as is always the case, in a portion of the forest where the trees were of great magnitude, and where there was little underwood.... I arrived there nearly two hours before sunset. Few Pigeons were then to be seen, but a great number of persons, with horses and wagons, guns and ammunition, had already established encampments on the borders. Two farmers from the vicinity of Russellsville, distant more than a hundred miles, had driven upwards of three hundred hogs to be fattened on the pigeons which were to be slaughtered. Here and there, the people employed in plucking and salting what had already been procured, were seen sitting in the midst of large piles of these birds. The dung lay several inches deep, covering the whole extent of the roosting place, like a bed of snow. Many trees two feet in diameter, I observed, were broken off at no great distance from the ground; and the branches of many of the largest and tallest had given way, as if the forest had been swept by a tornado. Everything proved to me that the number of birds resorting to this part of the forest must be immense beyond conception. As the period of their arrival approached, their foes anxiously prepared to receive them. Some were furnished with iron-pots containing sulphur, others with torches of pine-knots, many with poles, and the rest with guns.... Suddenly there burst forth a general cry of "Here they come!" The noise which they made, though yet distant, reminded me of a hard gale at sea, passing through the rigging of a close-reefed vessel. As the birds arrived and passed over me, I felt a current of air that surprised me. Thousands were soon knocked down by the pole-men.

Trillium bloom along a branch of the Pigeon River in the Great Smoky Mountains National Park in Tennessee.

The birds continued to pour in. The fires were lighted, and a magnificent, as well as wonderful and almost terrifying, sight presented itself. The Pigeons, arriving by the thousands, alighted everywhere, one above another, until solid masses ... were formed on the branches all round. Here and there the perches gave way under the weight with a crash, and falling to the ground, destroyed hundreds of the birds beneath, forcing down the dense groups with which every stick was loaded. It was a scene of uproar and confusion. I found it quite useless to speak, or even to shout to those persons who were nearest to me. Even the reports of the guns were seldom heard, and I was made aware of the firing only by seeing the shooters reloading.

No one dared venture within the line of devastation.... The uproar continued the whole night....

—John James Audubon,
Ornithological Biography, *1830-35.*

How the Rabbit Got His Beautiful Coat

A Cherokee Myth

The animals were of different sizes and wore coats of various colors and patterns. Some wore long fur and others wore short. Some had rings on their tails, and some had no tails at all. Some had coats of brown, others of black or yellow. They were always disputing about their good looks, so at last they agreed to hold a council to decide who had the finest coat.

They had heard a great deal about the Otter, who lived so far up the creek that he seldom came down to visit the other animals. It was said that he had the finest coat of all, but no one knew just what it was like, because it was a long time since anyone had seen him. They did not even know exactly where he lived—only the general direction; but they knew he would come to the council when word got out.

Now the Rabbit wanted the verdict for himself, so when it began to look as if it might go to the Otter he studied up a plan to cheat him out of it. He asked a few sly questions until he learned what trail the Otter would take to get to the council place. Then, without saying anything, he went on ahead and after four days' travel he met the Otter and knew him at once by his beautiful coat of soft dark-brown fur. The Otter was glad to see him and asked him where he was going. "O," said the Rabbit, "the animals sent me to bring you to the council; because you live so far away they were afraid you mightn't know the road." The Otter thanked him, and they went on together.

They traveled all day toward the council ground, and at night the Rabbit selected the camping place, because the Otter was a stranger in that part of the country, and cut down bushes for beds and fixed

The Little Pigeon River near the head of the Ramsay Cascades Trail in the Great Smoky Mountains National Park in Tennessee.

everything in good shape. The next morning they started on again. In the afternoon the Rabbit began to pick up wood and bark as they went along and to load it on his back. When the Otter asked what this was for the Rabbit said it was that they might be warm and comfortable at night. After a while, when it was near sunset, they stopped and made their camp.

Rhododendron bloom along the Alum Cave Bluffs Trail in the Great Smoky Mountains National Park in Tennessee.

When supper was over the Rabbit got a stick and shaved it down to a paddle. The Otter wondered and asked again what that was for.

"I have good dreams when I sleep with a paddle under my head," said the Rabbit.

When the paddle was finished the Rabbit began to cut away the bushes so as to make a clean trail down to the river. The Otter wondered more and more and wanted to know what this meant.

Said the Rabbit, "This place is called Ditatlaskiyi [The Place Where It Rains Fire]. Sometimes it rains fire here, and the sky looks a little that way tonight. You go to sleep and I'll sit up and watch, and if the fire does come, as soon as you hear me shout, you run and jump into the river. Better hang your coat on a limb over there, so it won't get burnt."

The Otter did as he was told, and they both doubled up to go to sleep, but the Rabbit kept awake. After a while the fire burned down to red coals. The Rabbit called, but the Otter was fast asleep and made no answer. In a little while he called again, but the Otter never stirred. Then the Rabbit filled the paddle with hot coals and threw them up into the air and shouted, "It's raining fire! It's raining fire!"

The hot coals fell all around the Otter and he jumped up. "To the water!" cried the Rabbit, and the Otter ran and jumped into the river, and he has lived in the water ever since.

The Rabbit took the Otter's coat and put it on, leaving his own instead, and went on to the council. All the animals were there, every one looking out for the Otter. At last they saw him in the distance, and they said one to the other, "The Otter is coming!" and sent one of the small animals to show him the best seat. They were all glad to see him and went up in turn to welcome him, but the Otter kept his head down, with one paw over his face. They wondered that he was so bashful, until the Bear came up and pulled the paw away, and there was the Rabbit with his split nose. He sprang up and started to run, when the Bear struck at him and pulled his tail off, but the Rabbit was too quick for them and got away.

—*James Mooney,*
***Myths of the Cherokee,** 1898.*

Wild flame azaleas bloom on Gregory Bald in the Great Smoky Mountains National Park, Tennessee/North Carolina. Reached only by hiker trails, this peak has the most prolific gardens of the wild shrub in the region. Due to mutations, the blooms range in color from pink and cream to yellow, deep orange, and red.

Wild azaleas and ferns at the edge of the forest on Gregory Bald (the mythical Rabbit Place), Tennessee/North Carolina.

The Great Rabbit, subject of the preceding story, was a mythical creature much larger than the rabbits of today. One of the great tricksters of native American mythology, he was extremely cunning, and although sometimes beaten at his own games by the fleet Deer or the steady Terrapin, he was always a worthy opponent. His exploits appear in the stories of many tribes. The Great Rabbit had his home in the high meadows and thickets of the Great Smoky Mountains' Gregory Bald, called "Rabbit Place" by the Cherokee. Here the rabbits had their townhouse. In old times the people could see him, and all the little rabbits were subject to him.

Origin of the Deer
A Shawnee Legend

Aa-pit-pa-taska, or the Yellow Sky, was the daughter of a Shawnee or Snake hunter. His lodge was not one of the handsomest in the village where it stood, but the paths leading to it were more beaten than those leading to any other, for the daughter of the hunter was a great favorite among the young men of her tribe. The exploits of those who sought her hand had no charms for her ear, and her tastes were strangely different from those common among women. She knew that she had not many years to live upon the earth, and her dreams had told her she was created for an unheard-of mission. There was a mystery about her being, and none could comprehend the meaning of her evening songs. On one condition alone did she avow her willingness to become a wife, and this was, that he who became her husband should never, under any circumstances, mention her name. If he did so, a sad calamity would befall him, and he would forever thereafter regret his thoughtlessness. By this decree was the love of one of her admirers greatly enhanced, and before the summer was gone the twain were married and dwelt in the same lodge.

Time flew on and the Yellow Sky sickened and died, and her last words were that her husband should never forget her admonition about breathing her name. The widower was very unhappy, and for five summers did he avoid his fellow-men, living in solitude, and wandering through the forest alone. The voices of autumn were now heard in the land, and the bereaved husband had, after his many journeyings, returned to the grave of his wife, which he found overgrown with briers and coarse weeds. For many moons had he neglected to protect the remains of his wife, and he now tried to atone for his wickedness by plucking up the briers and covering the grave with a soft sod. In doing this he was discovered by a stranger Indian, who asked him whose grave it was of which he was taking so much care? "It is the grave," said he, "of Aa-pit-pa-taska;" and hardly had the forbidden name (which he thoughtlessly uttered)

A white-tail deer amid late summer goldenrod at the edge of the forest.

A young doe browsing along the Appalachian Trail between Clingman's Dome and Siler's Bald in the Great Smoky Mountains National Park, Tennessee/North Carolina.

passed from his lips, before he fell to the earth in a spasm of great pain. The sun was setting, and his bitter moans echoed far through the gloomy woods, even until the darkness settled upon the world.

Morning came, and near the grave of the Yellow Sky a large buck was quietly feeding. It was the unhappy husband, whom the Great Spirit had thus changed. The trotting of a wolf was heard in the brake, and the deer pricked up his ears. One moment more, and the wolf started after the deer. The race was very long and painful, but the deer finally escaped. And thus from a man came into existence

Hen Wallow Falls, Great Smoky Mountains National Park, Tennessee.

the beautiful deer, or mu-rat-si; and because of the foolishness of this man, in not remembering his wife's words, the favorite animal of the Shawnee has ever been at the mercy of the wolf.

—Charles Lanman,
Adventures in the Wilds of the United States and British American Provinces, *1856.*

View from the Cliff Tops on Mount Le Conte, Great Smoky Mountains.

Coneflowers (yellow) and Bee Balm/Oswego Tea (red) bloom on route of the Appalachian Trail between Clingman's Dome and Siler's Bald, Great Smoky Mountains, Tennessee/North Carolina.

September 10, 1887:
    Escaped from a heap of uncordial kindness to the generous bosom of the woods. After a few miles of level ground... covered up like a tunnel by overarching oaks. ...adjusted to every slope and curve by the hands of Nature—the most sublime and comprehensive picture that ever entered my eyes....

—John Muir,
A Thousand-Mile Walk to the Gulf, 1887.

Ramsay Cascades, reached by hiker path, Great Smoky Mountains, Tennessee.

Autumn leaves collect in pool beside the Chimney Tops Trail, Great Smoky Mountains National Park, Tennessee.

The view toward Mount Le Conte from Clingman's Dome, Great Smoky Mountains National Park, Tennessee/North Carolina.

September 18, 1887:
 Up the mountain on the state line. The scenery is far grander than any I ever before beheld. The view extends from the Cumberland Mountains on the north far into Georgia and North Carolina to the south, an area of about five thousand square miles. Such an ocean of wooded, waving, swelling mountain beauty and grandeur is not to be described.
               —John Muir,
            A Thousand-Mile Walk to the Gulf, 1887.

The Fall of Fort Loudoun

During the conflict now remembered as the French and Indian War, in 1756, an army of 200 men from the South Carolina colony began building a long-promised fort in the Overhill Cherokee dominion. Solicited by the old chiefs, initially it was intended to cement trading relations and keep the loyalties of the Cherokee. It did not turn out as planned.

Fort Loudoun was built on a hill overlooking the Little Tennessee River just upstream from its junction with the Tellico River. Bureaucratic bungling, poor communications, and long-standing distrust on both sides led to the demise of the remote garrison in less than four years.

In one incident a Cherokee war party was returning home from duty with the British forces through Virginia. They had been denied their horses by the stable master for lack of an interpreter and, according to their customs, appropriated others found roaming on their walk home. White owners of the mounts took exception to having their property commandeered, and killed a number of the party. According to the Cherokee "blood law," all whites were then liable for the lost lives, and they took their revenge on unsuspecting North Carolina settlers.

Following this, a peace delegation was imprisoned at Fort Prince George in the South Carolina foothills. When one of the officers at the fort was lured outside and ambushed, all the hostages were slain. Full-scale war then erupted and the Cherokee laid siege to Fort Loudoun. A relief army of 1,500 British troops, along with Chickasaw and Catawba warriors, invaded the mountains from the east, burning Indian villages and crops en route; but near present-day Franklin, North Carolina, they were ambushed and forced to turn back to Charleston. Cherokee warriors at the battle boasted that they had scalped so many in the battle that their hands were sore from the work. As an added insult, one brave claimed that although he had cooked one of his enemies, and had intended to eat him, he had found the meat too salty.

The isolated defenders of Fort Loudoun survived for a time by eating their dogs and horses, and with food supplied by their Cherokee wives, but were then forced to surrender. Occupants of the fort were to retain only enough small arms and ammunition for the march back to the eastern settlements in exchange for safe conduct out of Cherokee country. Apparently, the agreement was not kept; or due to misunderstandings, the retreating party was attacked as they broke camp the second morning of the march, where Cane Creek enters the Tellico River. Many of the party were killed and scalped in the exchange, the rest captured. The leader of the troop, Captain Paul Demere, was brutally tortured and scalped alive, before having his arms and legs cut off. His tormentors filled his mouth with dirt, to fill his hunger for land, and taunted him as the "Dirt Captain." Historians note that Fort Loudoun was the only British-manned fort to fall to American Indians.

Indian victories in Appalachia were short-lived. With the French defeated, the British were intent on punishing the Cherokee, and attacked in spite of pleas of peace delegations. Sweeping through the Tuckasegee, Oconoluftee, Nantahala, and Cheoah Rivers, the country was devastated, with only scorched earth remaining in the army's wake. Then a peace treaty was concluded, including more land concessions.

During the interlude between wars, efforts at self-government began in the new settlements along the Watauga, Holston, and Nolichucky Rivers, as agitation for independence grew in the colonies. Land purchases and treaties were made with the Indians without benefit of official approval. Richard Henderson purchased a vast tract from the Cherokee that included most of Kentucky and the Cumberland area of Tennessee for his Transylvania Company. He set Daniel Boone and a crew of axe men to clearing the Wilderness Road to open up the country beyond Cumberland Gap to settlement. The Cherokee, who claimed the area as part of their traditional hunting grounds, knew it was also claimed by the Shawnee, Delaware, and others. This may account for the bitter remarks of Dragging Canoe, opposed to any concessions to the whites, when he called the ceded lands a "dark and bloody ground," apparently delighted that there was certain difficulty ahead for the settlers. His ambiguous statement has also been interpreted as a curse on the land—a curse realized in battles with the Shawnee and their allies, and again two centuries later when swarms of agents of the eastern "robber barons" began their advance on the mountain heartland. Sometimes through deception and fraud, but usually with the cooperation of gullible mountaineers unaware of the heritage they were signing away, great boundaries of timber and mineral rights were taken for little more than Henderson had given the Indians. Dragging Canoe had warned that to sell the earth would impoverish the Indians, since the paltry sums given would quickly be spent and then they would have nothing. His warning was not heeded by his people, nor by later stewards of the land.

Immediately preceding and during the American Revolution, pressure from white settlers, war, and smallpox decimated the Indian bands along the eastern slope of the mountains. Largest of the Appalachian tribes, the Cherokee were pushed from their eastern boundaries. The Little Tennessee and Hiwassee valley towns became the center of the nation. Traditionally the stronghold of the "Overhill" Cherokee, their villages dotted their banks from the highlands of North Carolina to the Tennessee River. The tenuous peace that had been bought by frequent land concessions had caused a bitter split within the tribe; and instigated by the British, many of the younger men took the warpath against the settlements. They had limited effect in battles against the entrenched communities along the Watuaga, Holston, Clinch, and Nolichucky Rivers, due in large part to a warning given by the tribe's Beloved Woman, Nancy Ward, who was trying to keep peace.

Armies totaling more than 5,000 men from the revolutionary governments responded by attacking from the Carolinas, Georgia, and Virginia and completely broke the resisting factions. Virtually all the Cherokee towns were obliterated, along with crops, orchards, and livestock. Men, women, and children unlucky enough to be

Chilhowie Lake with late summer wildflowers on the Little Tennessee River, the historic domain of the Overhill Cherokee.

caught were indiscriminately killed or sold into slavery. Much of the nation was reduced to eating roots and berries and hiding out in the mountains to escape. Following this catastrophe the dissident elements within the tribe moved down the Tennessee Valley to become the Chickamauga faction of the nation and occupied towns in southeastern Tennessee, northern Georgia, and Alabama. They remained hostile until defeated in 1815 by a volunteer army from the young state of Tennessee.

During this era, when the frontier moved west to the Cumberland and Kentucky, through stealth and deception the bloodletting could erupt in any Indian village or valley or hillside farm without warning; and as hatred between the races grew, the feverish rage of vengeance fell on the guilty and innocent alike. Few Indian or settler cabins escaped the mythical "Raven Mocker's" death call in the carnage.

The Tellico River near its junction with Cane Creek, site of the battle between Cherokee warriors and retreating British troops from Fort Loudoun.

The Kingdom of Paradise

Attempts were made by several Indian leaders to resist the tide of immigrants westward, but the Gods or fate seemed to always frustrate their attempts. Another effort to unite the tribes around the Appalachians in concerted resistance to the white advancement was mounted by a German intellect, Gotlieb Christian Priber.

Priber was an enigmatic figure. He arrived among the Cherokee around 1736 and adopted their dress, language, and lifestyle. He advocated a confederacy of Indian tribes to oppose the European intruders and to promote the establishment of a "Kingdom of Paradise." This domain was to be open to all who would accept communal ownership of property, equality of the sexes, and other utopian principles advocated by others more than a century later. He quickly mastered the Cherokee language and gained the confidence of the Indian leaders. A capital was established at Greater Tellico (in today's East Tennessee) with Priber as chief adviser to the Cherokee leaders. He was charged with being a French agent by the British authorities and was eventually arrested en route to Fort Toulouse, Alabama (then French territory). He died in English captivity, and his journals and dictionary of the Cherokee language were lost. It is probable that rather than being an agent of either the English or French, he tried to play the European powers against each other.

The Little Tennessee River, Chilhowie Lake, East Tennessee.

Bird-foot violets bloom in the Tellico District of Cherokee National Forest, East Tennessee.

September 19, 1887:

My path all today led me along the leafy banks of the Hiwassee, a most impressive mountain river. Its channel is very rough, as it crosses the edges of upturned rock strata, some of them standing at right angles, or glancing off obliquely to right and left. Thus a multitude of short, resounding cataracts are produced, and the river is restrained from the headlong speed due to its volume and in inclination of its bed.

All the larger streams of uncultivated countries are mysteriously charming and beautiful, whether flowing in mountains or through swamps and plains. Their channels are interestingly sculptured, far more so than the grandest architectural works of man. The finest of the forests are usually found along their banks, and in the multitude of falls and rapids the wilderness finds a voice. Such a river is the Hiwassee, with its surface broken to a thousand sparking gems, and its forest walls vine-draped and flowery as Eden. And how fine the songs it sings!

—John Muir,
A Thousand-Mile Walk to the Gulf, 1887.

Wild azaleas, with blossoms as sweet smelling as honeysuckle, bloom beside the John Muir Trail along the Hiwassee River in East Tennessee.

An early fall view along the Hiwassee River in East Tennessee, a scene similar to that witnessed by conservationist John Muir as he walked through the region.

John Muir was one of America's best known naturalists. In his book, **A Thousand-Mile Walk to the Gulf**, the journal of his first long trek is given. He began the journey at Louisville, Kentucky, and walked through town, following his compass south, without speaking to a soul. His route was through parts of Kentucky, Tennessee, North Carolina, and Georgia.

"My plan was simply to push on in a general southward direction by the wildest, leafiest, and least trodden way I could find, promising the greatest extent of virgin forest. Folding my map, I shouldered my little bag and plant press and strode away among the old Kentucky oaks, rejoicing in splendid visions of pines and palms and tropic flowers in glorious array, not, however, without a few cold shadows of loneliness, although the great oaks seemed to spread their arms in welcome."

After reaching Savannah he went by boat to Florida, then across the state on foot to reach the Gulf of Mexico. Although many landmarks are given in his journal, his exact route is not known. The walk is commemorated by foot trails along the Cumberland River, in the Big South Fork National Recreation Area, and along a part of the Hiwassee River. His walk probably joined the Hiwassee farther upstream from today's commemorative path, with much of the route now under the waters of Apalachia Lake. Following this adventure, Muir moved to California and eventually founded the Sierra Club.

The Race Between the Crane and the Hummingbird
A Cherokee Myth

The Hummingbird and the Crane were both in love with a pretty woman. She preferred the Hummingbird, who was as handsome as the Crane was awkward, but the Crane was so persistent that in order to get rid of him she finally told him he must challenge the other to a race and she would marry the winner. The Hummingbird was so swift—almost like a flash of lightning—and the Crane so slow and heavy, that she felt sure the Hummingbird would win. She did not know the Crane could fly all night.

They agreed to start from her house and fly around the circle of the world to the beginning, and the one who came in first would marry the woman. At the word the Hummingbird darted off like an arrow and was out of sight in a moment, leaving his rival to follow heavily behind. He flew all day, and when evening came and he stopped to roost for the night he was far ahead. But the Crane flew steadily all night long, passing the Hummingbird soon after midnight and going on until he came to a creek and stopped to rest about daylight. The Hummingbird woke up in the morning and flew on again, thinking how easily he would win the race, until he reached the creek and there found the Crane spearing tadpoles, with his long bill, for breakfast. He was very much surprised and wondered how this could have happened, but he flew swiftly by and soon left the Crane out of sight again.

The Crane finished his breakfast and started on, and when evening came he kept on as before. This time it was hardly midnight when he passed the Hummingbird asleep on a limb, and in the morning he had finished his breakfast before the other came up. The next day he gained a little more, and on the fourth day he was spearing tadpoles for dinner when the Humming bird passed him. On the fifth and sixth days it was late in the afternoon before the Hummingbird came up, and on the morning of the seventh day the Crane was a

Geese take flight in the Hiwassee Wildlife Refuge, near the confluence of the Hiwassee and Tennessee Rivers.

whole night's travel ahead. He took his time at breakfast and then fixed himself up nicely as he could at the creek and came in at the starting place where the woman lived, early in the morning. When the Hummingbird arrived in the afternoon he found he had lost the race, but the woman declared she would never have such an ugly fellow as the Crane for a husband, so she stayed single.

—James Mooney,
Myths of the Cherokee*,*
1898.

A great blue heron watches its nest in the Hiwassee Wildlife Refuge, Tennessee.

Heron rookery on an island in the upper Chickamauga Lake, in the Hiwassee Wildlife Refuge, Tennessee.

The Coming of Death
A Cherokee Tradition

In the cosmology of most woodland tribes, the Sun was a male spirit and the Moon female. In the full moon of the Iroquois an old woman could be seen weaving pelts together for a rug, but each month her cat would unravel her work and she would have to begin again. The Creek and other southern tribes saw the Moon as a much younger woman who would disappear for a few days each month to tryst with the Sun or other sky spir-

The sun rises over the Blue Ridge in a view from Balsam Knob in the Shining Rock area of Western North Carolina.

its. But according to the Cherokee ancients, the Sun was a cranky old woman.

Somewhere in the vastness of time before time, the Sun and the Moon and the sky world came to be. These were followed by the creation of the animals, people, and all other things. Exactly how everything should be had not yet been decided, so at that time people might live forever.

As a young woman the Sun had had a playful nature. She had many suitors, but Her favorite would only come courting at night when no moon was in the sky. Since it was always so dim when He came, She became obsessed with discovering His identity. One night when He came calling, She felt His face sympathetically and said, "Oh dear, your face is so cold, you must have suffered from the wind."

But, unknown to Him, She had rubbed Her hands with charcoal. The next time the Moon rose in the east He had dark spots on His face and She knew Her night visitor had been Her brother. Since that time, due to His embarrassment, He has always stayed as far from Her in the sky as possible, or when He approaches Her in the west He is reduced to just a sliver.

Now, as the years passed, the Sun came to hate the people on the Earth because they could never look straight at Her without frowning. She said to Her brother, the Moon, "My grandchildren are ugly; they grin all over their faces when they look at me." But the Moon said, "I like my younger brothers; I think they are very handsome"—because they always smiled pleasantly when they saw Him at night.

This made the Sun jealous, and She planned to kill all the people. She sent down such sultry rays that there was fever and people died by the hundreds.

Some of the tribe's most powerful conjurers went for help to the Little Men, who said the only way to save themselves was to kill the Sun.

The Little Men made medicine and changed two of the Shaman into snakes and told them what to do. It seems that each day the Sun stopped in Her journey along the sky's arch for lunch at Her daughter's house. Since the Sun's daughter lived nearby they decided to station themselves near her door so that the next day when the old Sun approached they could bite and kill Her before She knew what was happening. Unfortunately, the daughter was bitten by mistake and she died.

The Sun was then so sad She would not come out any more. The people stopped dying from the heat, but now the world was always dark and getting bitterly cold. The Little Men were again asked for advice. This time it was decided that in order to get the Sun to come out again they must bring Her daughter back from the ghost country.

Seven brave warriors were selected to travel to the darkening land in the west. Each was given a sourwood rod that had magical powers, and they were told to touch the girl with them as she danced with the other spirit people. When they reached the Spirit World they found all the ghosts dancing. Being careful to stand outside the circle of dancers, each of the travelers touched the dancing girl with their magical staffs as she passed. The other spirits never seemed to notice what was happening; and on the seventh touch, the girl's spirit fell to the ground. Then they placed her into a special box for the return trip.

The Little Men had told them not to lift the lid of the box for anything.

But on the return journey the girl came back to life and pleaded and pleaded to be let out of the box. At first the men remembered their instructions and ignored her cries, but as they neared the village they feared she was about to suffocate and just cracked the lid enough for her to get air. At that moment there was a flutter and something flew past them; then they noticed a red bird nearby in the thicket.

When they opened the box at the village it was empty, so they knew that the red bird was the Sun's daughter, whose spirit had escaped. With it they had also lost the ability to return their friends and families from the ghost country. All possible means were resorted to in order to bring back life, but in vain. The whole race was doomed to follow, not only to death, but to misery afterwards, so that now someone who dies can never be called back.

The Sun had been glad when they started to the ghost country, but when She saw that they had failed

The sun burst through clouds in a view from Cold Mountain in the Shining Rock Wilderness of North Carolina.

to return with Her daughter, She grieved and cried, "My daughter, my daughter," and wept until Her tears made a flood upon the Earth. Fearing that the whole world would be drowned, they held another council and sent their handsomest young men and women to amuse Her. They danced before the Sun and sang their best songs, but for a long time She kept Her face covered and paid no attention, until at last the drummer, just by chance, suddenly changed the beat. She lifted up Her face and was so pleased that She forgot Her grief and smiled on the Earth again. But since that time, the days of each person have been numbered and to each a share of grief must be endured.

—Retold from James Mooney,
***Myths of the Cherokee,** 1898.*

The Mountain People
A Cherokee Legend

Long ago there was a Cherokee village on the French Broad River [near today's Brevard, North Carolina] called Kanasta. One day two strangers, who looked in no way different from other Cherokee, came into the settlement and made their way to the chief's house. After the first greetings were over, the chief asked them from what town they had come, thinking them from one of the western settlements, but they said, "We are of your people and our town is close at hand, but you have never seen it. Here you have wars and sickness, with enemies on every side, and after a while a stronger enemy will come to take your country from you. We are always happy, and we have come to invite you to live with us in our town over there," and they pointed toward Pilot Knob on the crest of the Blue Ridge Mountains.

"We do not live forever, and do not always find game when we go for it, for the game belongs to Tsukalu, who lives inside Tennessee bald, but we have peace always and need not think of danger. We go now, but if your people will live with us let them fast seven days, and we shall come then to take them."

The chief called his people together into the townhouse to hold a council over the matter and decided at last to go with the strangers. They got all their property ready for moving and then went again into the townhouse and began their fast. They fasted six days, and on the morning of the seventh, before the sun was high, they saw a great company coming along the trail from the mountains, led by the two men who had stopped with the chief. They took up a part of the goods to be carried, and the two parties started back together. There was one man from another town visiting at Kanasta, and he went along with the rest.

When they came to the mountain, the two guides led the way into a cave, which opened out like a great door in the side of the rock. Inside they found an open country and a town, with houses ranged in two long rows from east to west. The mountain people lived in the houses on the south side, and they had made ready the other houses for the newcomers, but even after all the people of Kanasta, with their children and belongings, had moved in, there were still a larger number of houses waiting ready for the next who might come. The mountain people told them that there was another town, of a different people, above them in the same mountain, and still farther above, at the very top, lived the Thunders.

Now all the people of Kanasta were settled in their new homes, but the man who had only been visiting with them wanted to go back to his own friends. Some of the mountain people wanted to prevent this, but the chief said, "No; let him go if he will, and when he tells his friends they may want to come, too. There is plenty of room for all."

Then he said to the man, "Go back and tell your friends that if they want to come and live with us and be always happy, there is a place here ready and waiting for them. Others of us live in Shining Rock, under Cold Mountain, and the high mountains all around, and if they would rather go to any of them it is all the same. We see you wherever you go and are with you in all your dances, but you can not see us unless you fast. If you want to see us, fast four days, and we will come and talk with you; and then if you want to live with us, fast again seven days, and we will come and take you." Then the chief led the man through the cave to the outside of the mountain and left him there, but when the man looked back he saw no cave, but only the solid rock.

—*Retold from James Mooney,*
***Myths of the Cherokee**, 1898.*

Sunset from Cold Mountain in the Shining Rock Wilderness of North Carolina.

Methodist Bishop Francis Asbury traveled extensively in the Appalachian Region during the last quarter of the eighteenth century preaching to all who would listen. On October 30, 1800, on a trip through the mountains, he made the following observation:

And here let me record the gracious dealings of God to my soul in this journey: I have had uncommon peace of mind, and spiritual consolations every day; not-withstanding the long rides I have endured, and the frequent privations of good water and proper food to which I have been subjected; to me the wilderness and the solitary places were made as the garden of God, and as the presence-chambers of the King of Kings and the Lord of Lords.

—**Journal of Bishop Francis Asbury**, 1800.

Blue Ridge Crest Area

A shimmering mosaic of mystic woods, clad in early summer hues of emerald, beckons with fluid-like coolness. Tree branches and leaves, rippling in a light breeze, break the blue-white flood of afternoon sunlight into waves of vibrating pulses, flashing here and there along the forest floor. Highlights spark and dance among lacy ferns. Slender grasses outline a carpeted footpath winding into a subtle, darker sylvan world beyond. Inside this lush haven of greens, mixed with golden wildflowers and somber tree trunks of gray, brown, and black, and accents of ice blue and lime algae and lichens, even the air and light seem supersaturated.

Slipping quietly into this natural landscape there is a feeling of peace and enhanced spirituality. Treading softly along the narrow path that has seen a procession of countless souls, one person is an insignificant detail in the parade of centuries. Climbing atop rocky pinnacles, unobstructed panoramas stretch to infinity, offering an illusion of uninterrupted mountains flowing to the horizon. In the foreground is a gently undulating sea

Kings Mountain National Battlefield, site of the battle of the Overmountain Men and British Loyalist troops under Colonel Patrick Ferguson, along the North Carolina/South Carolina border.

of forest and hills, sharply defined with dark greens and black, then colors erode as an atmospheric blue washes over succeeding ridges in a stepped scale of tones ebbing from rich cyan, turquoise, and aqua to the softened shades of worn denim near the white rim dividing land and sky. But even this ancient spine of the Blue Ridge has been transformed many times.

Once upon a time in this fairy tale land, these gentle slopes were the domain of a race of Giants and Little People who had God-like powers. Mortals, such as the Indian tribes living

Flame azaleas line the Appalachian Trail on Blood Mountain, Georgia.

A waterfall in the Raven Cliffs Wilderness Area of North Georgia.

around the Southern mountains, had evolved an intricate system of beliefs and accommodations that respected the forest spirits and all creation. The upper and lower worlds existed simultaneously with the present physical existence, and in the mountain recesses were mysterious passages between. It was believed that all animated things had a spirit, and even stones and trees sometimes moved or spoke. All beings were honored. Fasting, ritual, and sacred formulas were used to seek guidance for the spiritual vision quest.

These older mystical perceptions of our relationships with the earth seem the more valid reality when standing in the lofty forest. Here the paths were created as much by passing deer as by mankind, and the only sounds are those of birds, insects, or falling water. Stepping from the tensions, fumes, raw nerves, and winding asphalt, behind groaning, overweight recreation vehicles, a walk along the soothing paths of the Appalachian highlands could be compared to visiting another world, or plane of being. Passing through a labyrinth of twisted laurel and hawthorn, factories, city sidewalks, and suburban shopping malls all seem otherworldly. We can step from one to the other almost magically.

Wild blueberry bushes and autumn colors line the Graveyard Fields Trail along the Blue Ridge Crest, North Carolina.